nd Sophie Anderson Philip Ardagh Yaba
ri Anthony Browne ... acy
Cowell Isabelle ... ams
ssman Matt Haig V... ne
M. Homes Nadine Ai... ten
an Kieran Neal Lay... es
alik James Mayhew Wyl Menmuir Kiran
is Sarah Moss Benjamin Myers Beverley
Chibundu Onuzo Onjali Q. Raúf Chris
Lorna Scobie Andy Shepherd Francesca
Stephens Colin Thubron Piers Torday
Weymouth Raynor Winn Emma Yarlett
nd Sophie Anderson Philip Ardagh Yaba
ri Anthony Browne Edward Carey Tracy
Cowell Isabelle Dupuy Inua Ellams
ssman Matt Haig Vashti Hardy Joanne
M. Homes Nadine Aisha Jassat Carster
Dan Kieran Neal Layton Huw Lewis-Jones
alik James Mayhew Wyl Menmuir Kiran
is Sarah Moss Benjamin Myers Beverley
Chibundu Onuzo Onjali Q. Raúf Chris
Lorna Scobie Andy Shepherd Francesca
Stephens Colin Thubron Piers Torday
Weymouth Raynor Winn Emma Yarlett
nd Sophie Anderson Philip Ardagh Yaba
ri Anthony Browne Edward Carey Tracy
Cowell Isabelle Dupuy Inua Ellams
ssman Matt Haig Vashti Hardy Joanne
M. Homes Nadine Aisha Jassat Carster
Dan Kieran Neal Layton Huw Lewis-Jones
alik James Mayhew Wyl Menmuir Kiran
is Sarah Moss Benjamin Myers Beverley
Chibundu Onuzo Onjali Q. Raúf Chris
Lorna Scobie Andy Shepherd Francesca
Stephens Colin Thubron Piers Torday
Weymouth Raynor Winn Emma Yarlett

Swallowed by a Whale

Swallowed by a Whale

How to Survive the Writing Life

Edited by
Huw Lewis-Jones

First published in 2020 by
The British Library
96 Euston Road
London NW1 2DB

ISBN 978 0 7123 5303 8

Compiled and edited by Huw Lewis-Jones
Text edited by Sarah Vernon-Hunt
Designed by Karin Fremer
Cover Artwork by Bill Bragg

Printed and bound in the Czech Republic by Findr

Fiction was invented the day
Jonah arrived home and told his wife
that he was three days late because
he had been swallowed by a whale.
GABRIEL GARCÍA MÁRQUEZ

CONTENTS

INTRODUCTION *Huw Lewis-Jones* - 8

ESCAPING
STORIES NOT ATOMS *Huw Lewis-Jones* - 12
WE NEED CANDLES *Chris Riddell* - 17
THIS IS WHAT I KNOW *Kwame Alexander* - 24
BE BRAVE *David Almond* - 30
THINK OF HARALD *Andy Riley* - 32

GOLDEN RULES I
Jim Al-Khalili - 36
Sophie Anderson - 38
Philip Ardagh - 41
Yaba Badoe - 45
Alex Bell - 47
Edward Carey - 49
Frank Cottrell-Boyce - 52
Cressida Cowell - 53
Inua Ellams - 55
Maz Evans - 57
Lev Grossman - 59
Matt Haig - 62
Vashti Hardy - 64

PICTURING
WRITE LIKE AN ANIMAL *Lorna Scobie* - 68
DRAW AND LOOK *Anthony Browne* - 72
TO THE TEMPLE *Piers Torday* - 74
A BLANK SHEET *James Mayhew* - 77
MATHEMATICAL *Harry Baker* - 80
THE SHAPE OF STARS *Emma Yarlett* - 81
NAIVETY IS GOOD *Helen Stephens* - 84

GOLDEN RULES II
Joanne Harris - 100
Michelle Harrison - 102
Philip Hoare - 104
A.M. Homes - 105
Nadine Aisha Jassat - 107
Catherine Johnson - 109
Huw Lewis-Jones - 111
Anthony McGowan - 114
Gregory Maguire - 117

Ayisha Malik - 120
Kiran Millwood Hargrave - 123
David Mitchell - 125
Benjamin Myers - 127

REFLECTING
THE WIDE WORLD Jan Morris - 132
BENEATH THE SURFACE Carsten Jensen - 135
A RED SUITCASE Onjali Q. Raúf - 137
CREATIVE PATHS Dan Kieran - 139
A LONG GAME Wyl Menmuir - 142
SOME SYMBOLS Sita Brahmachari - 144
READ SOME MORE Sarah Moss - 146
A FEW WORDS Raynor Winn - 148
ROLL THE DICE Tom Gauld - 151

GOLDEN RULES III
Beverley Naidoo - 156
Sally Nicholls - 158
Paraic O'Donnell - 161
Chibundu Onuzo - 163
Michael Rosen - 165
Jacob Ross - 166
Andy Shepherd - 170
Francesca Simon - 173
Chitra Soundar - 175
Colin Thubron - 176
Novuyo Rosa Tshuma - 177
Irvine Welsh - 179
Adam Weymouth - 180

BEGINNING
BEAUTIFUL PLANET Neal Layton - 184
FORGET THE ODDS Andy Stanton - 190
FESTIVAL QUESTIONS Simon Garfield - 192
WELL-WORN PHRASES Tracy Chevalier - 195
ABOUT TO BE Isabelle Dupuy - 197
BANISH THE DARK Thomas Keneally - 199
TELLING STORIES Huw Lewis-Jones - 202

Biographies - 206
Acknowledgments - 221
Further Reading - 222

INTRODUCTION
Huw Lewis-Jones

'Start', Kurt Vonnegut would often tell his students, 'as close to the end as possible.'

Getting started is hard. Even the most successful authors find writing difficult and have endured rejection and setback on their journey to bestseller fame and fortune. The good news, however, is that there are many ways to write. But just how do writers make up stories? How is fiction invented? How do they begin? And how do they keep on going?

Being a writer frequently feels like you've been swallowed by a whale: engulfed by difficulties of your own making. The solitude, the debt, the anxiety. A future uncertain at best. Solitary confinement. A deadline creeping closer by the day. Doubting yourself, and still the blank page looms. There's not much sunshine inside this whale of yours and sometimes you feel like you're losing the plot. Struggling against oblivion. And yet, when at last the words come and inspiration strikes – when the whale is finally escaped – it can be a joyous occupation. It's intoxicating. There is hope.

But it is rarely easy. So why on earth do writers do it? And why do they come back for more? In this specially commissioned anthology, more than sixty accomplished authors share secrets and insights into their writing lives – their inspirations, methods, wild ideas and daily routines; the pleasure and the pain in achieving their literary goals; how they started out and how they hope to continue. They outline some golden rules for staying on track and talk candidly about what goes wrong as well as right. There are novelists, poets, biographers and children's writers, illustrators, campaigners, teachers, mothers, husbands, an entrepreneur turned surfboard shaper, a quantum physicist, an opera librettist and a Laureate who loves dragons. All writers.

There are emerging talents here alongside much-loved authors whose books have sold in millions. Each reflects in their own way on the creative process and the compulsion to write. Naturally, their advice is theirs to give, and so often differs. Each tells their own tale. How to find inspiration? How to get the words right? How to cope with writer's block? How to ignore accountants? How to handle bad reviews? How to become a better reader? Pencil or computer? Inside or out? And where do the good ideas really come from?

This is a new compendium of honest writing advice, it's a gathering of home truths and survival tactics: a meditation on the art of making things up for a living. In reading this collection, aspiring writers can beware and be encouraged too. There is clearly no single or simple answer to the question of how stories are created, but this book should help you get closer to a solution that works for you. It might just save you from being swallowed entirely, never to be seen again. Sometimes you also have to allow yourself to be consumed by the whale, and somewhere in that darkness find your story.

Many authors actually loathe writing. All love having written. For most, whether beginner or veteran, it is hard to get started and equally tough to continue. It's usually unglamorous, frequently precarious, but the rewards are there if you work at it, and get lucky. When all is said and done, the best way to become a writer is to knuckle down and *write*. Or, at least for now, sit awhile with this book and keep reading. As Dorothy Parker put it: 'Writing is the art of applying the ass to the seat.'

ΕSCAPING

STORIES NOT ATOMS
Huw Lewis-Jones

A few years ago I made an atlas. Inside were some of the great maps of English fiction, from Middle-earth to Narnia, Treasure Island and Earthsea. Legendary literary places. Each of these cherished invented worlds, and more, began in stories their creators told themselves and shared with their families and friends. They sometimes started with a map long before words were set down on the page, in sketching and thinking, dreaming, playing. The first map in the atlas was drawn in 1826 by a girl who was then just nine years old; it is so tiny it could fit in the palm of your hand. It was made by Charlotte Brontë, who would later become one of the greatest writers in the English language. She wrote herself a story and placed a map at the front.

Every book has a map woven within its pages. It's an invisible chart of where, when, how and why the book was written: a landscape of creation, showing where the story had its origins, where the writer toiled over the manuscript, where it was completed, printed and published, and even where it was then translated, adapted, reworked and reimagined. Quite naturally, authors also reshape this terrain when they look back and retell their own stories of how they became writers. Literary geography is personal cartography as much as it is a global activity.

But where do stories themselves *begin*? Most books start with a single idea – the handful of notes that in time become a chorus. Some emerge in an event, or in the memory of an event, and their life journey starts the very moment they are spoken or shared for the first time. Though each writer has their own methods, many are the same. The stories they tell begin with half-thoughts – the sense of a character, an idea of a place, a view of an emerging scene – which are then nurtured by a great deal of hard work and patience. In time, in the retelling and the rewriting, these gathered thoughts may grow into a structured story and find a new life when released into the world and published as book. But many more stories are never printed. For stories don't need to be confined to paper alone.

The stars in the night sky are surely one of earliest and greatest sources of wonder for stories, and have launched more journeys and inspired more tales around a campfire or a ship's wheel than any other. Ptolemy, in the second century AD, was not the first to create stories of gods, dragons and countless other known and unknown beasts, but he was among the first to draw them upon the night sky in a combination of myth and mathematics. Legends from Assyria, Babylonia and other ancient civilizations found their way to Ptolemy's ear, and he wove elements from each into the tapestry of his celestial chart, and in the stories he would share with those willing to listen.

Precisely how these stories were mapped on the night sky, we will never know, nor need we know. Save that they did. This is John Berger, writing in 1984:

> *Lying on our backs, we look up at the night sky. This is where stories began, under the aegis of that multitude of stars which at night filch certitudes and sometimes return them as faith. Those who first invented and then named the constellations were storytellers. Tracing an imaginary line between a cluster of stars gave them an image and an identity. The stars threaded on that line were like events threaded on a narrative. Imagining the constellations did*

> not of course change the stars, nor did it change the black
> emptiness that surrounds them. What it changed was the
> way people read the night sky.

Or, as the American poet Muriel Rukeyser put it so well: 'the universe is made of stories, not of atoms'.

Writers and storytellers still like to venture outside to find the words they need. It might mean looking up to the sky, or getting lost in a busy city, or merely sitting still and emptying the mind. For Joseph Heller, for example, new stories entered his head when walking his dog, brushing his teeth or simply lying down. He explained, 'they come to me in the course of a sort of controlled daydream'. Of course, not all stories have such gentle beginnings. Many books are born in heartache and upheaval, violence and suffering. It is no surprise then that in crafting new truths from very real horrors, writers may try to salvage some peace in which to do it – to create a quiet, secure place to revisit and work their way through such traumas.

Rudyard Kipling liked long walks in the countryside. When the right words refused to come, he strode outside, developing sentences as he moved, a fresh-air process he called 'hatching'. Back inside, beyond the creative chaos of his desk – his 'dunghill' – in the corner of his study was a day-bed, where he would lie down and give himself time to nurture new thoughts and dwell on them in silence. Towards the end of his life he explained this as listening for the *daemon* that informed his craft, knowing that many things simply take time: to write, you need to 'drift, wait, obey'.

For other writers the process is much more painful, more sweat and tears, and less romanticized in the retelling. Great writers often come from the margins. The hardships they encounter – the whales they endure and outlast – forge them as writers. Joseph Conrad, a pioneer of modernism, began his journey as an author in improbable circumstances. Born in 1857, the son of Polish nationalists who were exiled to a swamp north of Moscow by the tsarist police, he was orphaned aged eleven, became a sailor and spent most of his youth working in the merchant navy roaming around the Indian Ocean. He attempted suicide by shooting himself in the chest, but the bullet missed his heart. Writing came many years later, after spotting an advert in a magazine calling for nautical yarns. He decided to have a go even though English was his third language and, despite an almost constant struggle, completed a novel just before the end of the century.

In later years Conrad fictionalized his own past, artfully reinventing it. Much of being a writer is pretty ordinary – normal life, working hard, long hours at a desk, with slim hope of success. Roald Dahl once said that being a successful writer meant having 'to keep your bottom on the chair', and by that he meant you have to *stick at it*. That is, writing every day, even when you feel you can't, when finding the right words is like wading through glue. 'For if you start getting into the habit of walking away when you're stuck, you'll never get it done.'

But it's also important to allow yourself time to dream ideas into being. To listen carefully to the small ideas that lead to a beginning. Nabokov called it 'the first little throb'. The inkling, or impulse, of the book you want to write that suddenly beats within you; the half-thought that soon takes over your life. Ideas for books come from many directions: in daydreams, yes, but also when taking a shower, standing in a queue, riding a bus or stuck in traffic on the way to the job that actually pays the bills. Good ideas also often emerge in enjoying another's work, for what better way to become a writer than in being a reader? But when that first idea, that first itch, arrives there is only one way to scratch it: you must begin to *write*.

Books begin in all places, at all times. Mary Shelley sparked her *Frankenstein* into life telling ghost stories in Switzerland. John Steinbeck found his great idea while working as a ranch hand in California. Thomas Malory wrote *Le Morte d'Arthur* while interned in Newgate prison. Jules Verne met Phileas Fogg when reading a newspaper in a Parisian cafe. E.B. White watched a spider in his shed in Maine daily weave its intricate web. In 1836, ten years after drawing her first little map, Charlotte Brontë explained her urge to become an author quite simply: 'I'm just going to write because I cannot help it.'

Gabriel García Márquez was driving to Acapulco with his family when he imagined the first line of a novel that would become his most famous work, *One Hundred Years of Solitude*. J.M. Barrie's Neverland shimmered into being when telling stories in a park. J.K. Rowling famously found her wizards while stuck on a crowded train. Kerouac bashed out his manuscript of *On the Road* fuelled on a diet of soup and coffee, taping together sheets of tracing paper into one long scroll to avoid reloading his typewriter every time he finished a page. After twenty days of nonstop writing, his wife kicked him out of the house, but he didn't slow up. When his draft was done it was 120 feet long. Or, so the story goes.

WE NEED CANDLES
Chris Riddell

SWALLOWED BY A
WHALE

IT IS NOT JONAH THAT I THINK OF
WHEN I THINK OF THE WHALE BUT GEPPETTO
IN SEARCH OF HIS CREATION...

IN THE BELLY OF THE BEAST
IN THAT CAVERNOUS
DARK

THE DOUBTS
ECHO AROUND
OUR HEADS...

WHICH IS WHY WE NEED
CANDLES,

LOTS OF CANDLES.

THESE ARE MY CANDLES...

DON'T THINK JUST DRAW

KEEP A SKETCHBOOK AND FILL THE PAGES WITH ANYTHING

DON'T BE AFRAID TO DO NOTHING... ALLOW TIME FOR IDEAS TO FORM...

KEEP YOUR NERVE, KEEP LIGHTING THE CANDLES AND

WAIT FOR THE LITTLE WOODEN BOY TO FIND YOU...

WHEN HE DOES, AND HE WILL,
MAKE A BONFIRE

AND WAIT FOR THE
BIG...

THIS IS WHAT I KNOW
Kwame Alexander

1. Sometimes, we need others to motivate us, to help us dream, to bounce ideas off, to rebound, to grow with. A team. A dream team ...

The book wasn't even my idea. See, I'd met a publisher at a summer writers' conference in New York City, and she and I got to talking about poetry for young people, which I didn't think there was enough of in classrooms. *Maybe*, she said, *you should consider writing something. You have the chops, the passion, and your voice is so deliciously muscular* (OK, maybe I added the delicious part). Maybe I should, I thought, arching my back and poking out my chest, literally. *In fact*, she continued, *you should write a novel, in verse, about a boy, who plays basketball.*

Now, I wasn't great at basketball (tennis was my competitive sport in high school), but I knew my way around a basketball court, and I thoroughly enjoyed watching it. If I write this book, will you publish it? I asked, intrigued, putting her on the spot. *I will most definitely ... consider publishing it.* That was all I needed to hear, but there was one problem: while I'd written fourteen books of poetry, I'd never written a novel. I knew how to create a compelling beginning, a middle and an end in a few stanzas, but not in a few hundred pages. Still, I wasn't going to let this opportunity escape. She'd opened the door, so I planned to walk right through it, not knowing what was on the other side. I said yes.

2. Champions learn from champions before they become champions. Study the great ones who played before you so you can 'pick-up' the things that worked and 'pass' on the things that didn't ...

The task was daunting. The blank page intimidated me. I didn't know where or how to begin. I had the will, but not the skill. So, I scoured my local library for a playbook that could guide me. I read every verse novel I could get my hands on, and stayed away from every verse novel that had anything to do with basketball. See, I needed to *borrow* craft without *stealing* content. *Out of the Dust* by Karen Hesse taught me about plot and character development. *Street Love* by Walter Dean Myers modelled rhythm and brevity. *All the Broken Pieces* by Ann E. Burg showed me an authentic boy's voice, and how to use sports as a metaphor. *Love That Dog* by Sharon Creech taught me about being concise and using white space. *The Way a Door Closes* by Hope Anita Smith was a case study in storytelling with weighty themes. These books had the answers I needed to begin writing with confidence. And, that's what I did.

3. You can't know what you don't know. Losing is an opportunity to get better, to learn what to do to win ...

I wrote every day. Five hours or so a day. For nine months. I submitted the novel to the publisher I'd met in New York City and got a quick rejection. The poems were good, the story was weak. I rewrote the novel. In six months. Another rejection. The story was better, but the characters weren't developed. I self-edited and rewrote and resubmitted, until finally I was told the novel simply wasn't working. But, I didn't know why. I didn't know what was wrong, and thus, I didn't know how to fix it. For three years' work, the only thing I had to show was a weak, two-hundred-plus-page unpublishable manuscript and no idea how to make it stronger. I needed help.

So, I googled: *Writing coach, novel-in-verse, poetry*. I found a few writers with the bona fides, but they were too costly for an out-of-work poet. So, I added *cheap* to my search and found a writer who'd taught poetry, written numerous books of poetry – a few novellas in verse – and most importantly only charged $800 for a manuscript review and edit. For the next eight months, she put me through a novel-in-verse boot camp – redlined my manuscript, modelled what my poems should look like, challenged me to get inside the mind and heart of my characters, gave me reading assignments, told me my crap was crap, praised my word choice, listened, read, laughed out loud and taught me things about storytelling that I simply didn't know. I'd finished it, and it was very good.

4. Never let anyone lower your goals. Others' expectations of you are determined by their limitations of life. In order to soar, you gotta believe the sky is your limit. Always shoot for the Sun ...

My first agent was a small, niche agent who tried to sell my novel to publishers, but just couldn't get any takers. We parted ways, but remained friends. My second agent was with one of the largest literary agencies in the world, so I knew that it was a matter of time before I was a critically acclaimed, bestselling author. Weekly, however, he relayed rejection after rejection to me, all the while still encouraging me to work on new stuff, which I did (half-heartedly). See, I really believed in my novel and needed to get that out into the world before I gave myself wholly and solely to a new story.

After a year and a half of staggering in this literary limbo, I ventured to New York to meet with my power agent, to get some guidance on why no publisher was interested in my masterpiece, to get some professional advice on next steps. It was a lovely day, the sun shining brilliant with possibility, when I sat down across from him in his thirty-second-floor corner office. So, what's up? I asked. What are publishers saying about the novel? *Well, Kwame*, he started, *truth is, I never sent your novel out to publishers.* What do you mean? *Kwame, it's poetry. And, as your agent, I didn't think it was a good move. It's not the kind of book you want to define your career.*

There's this story about an enslaved African named Henry Box Brown who escaped American slavery by climbing into a crate and literally mailing himself to freedom (that's commitment!). But, here's the thing that people never talk about. What about the dude that Henry convinced to nail the crate shut so he wouldn't be detected? What if that guy had decided that it wasn't a good move for Henry to attempt to go postal (I couldn't resist)? I believe it's crucial that we surround ourselves with the right team, with people who share our vision, who we trust with our dreams, who say yes to our possibilities. So, I fired the agent.

5. Dribble, fake, shoot, miss. Dribble, fake, shoot, miss. Dribble, fake, shoot, miss. Dribble, fake, shoot, SWISH!

Industry rules say you shouldn't fire your agent – let alone two of them – or you'll develop a bad reputation. I was almost five years into my writerly journey as a novelist, and I was on my third agent. I made it clear to her that selling my novel was first priority, and she assured me that we were on the same page. Six months into our relationship, she sold it. A year later my debut novel hit the shelves and I hit the road, promoting it tirelessly in cities across the United States. Over the next year, students, boys in particular, began picking up the book and reading it. And then girls started reading this book that all the boys were raving about. Then, teachers and librarians were next to pick it up. And, before you know it, the buzz grew tremendously, and my little novel started getting mentioned in mock award blogs and in review magazines.

Then 2 February 2015 happened. I was fast asleep when my phone rang at 7.16 a.m. Startled by the Tears for Fears ringtone, I jumped up and answered it. *Hello, I'm calling from the Newbery Committee*, the caller said, *to tell you that* … I immediately knew this was going to be a good call … *to tell you that* … I started thinking about all the rejections and all the NOs … *to tell you that your novel, The Crossover, is the winner of the Newbery Medal for the Most Distinguished Contribution to American Literature for Children.*

Now, this is what I know:

Say yes.

Be tenacious in your art.

Believe in yourself even when it seems that no one else does.

Surround yourself with the right team, with people who support you, who are equally – if not more – passionate and ambitious.

Create your own play.

Honour the ones who've come before you.

Honour the greatness that is you.

Practise.

Face defeat.

Rebound.

Expect to win.

Win.

BE BRAVE
David Almond

Be brave. Just do it. Just write. We're imperfect beings in an imperfect world. So be imperfect. Be messy. Make mistakes. Get a notebook, get pens and pencils, magic markers, crayons. Each blank page is an invitation, a new landscape, a field of possibilities. Writing is a physical act. Move your hand. Make marks. Scribble, doodle, draw, write, experiment and play. Plunge happily into a beautiful creative mess. Be free. Allow your stories, poems, songs, plays to come to life on your pages.

Compose on the computer screen. Turn the mess in your mind and the mess in your notebooks into the beautiful order of straight lines and pages. Create a title page from the very start, even if you know it's the wrong title. Write in page view – as if by magic, the computer shows the next page appearing as you write. Have a running header with the title, your name and the page number. Print out your work, hold it together with staples or bulldog clips. Scribble on it, throw away, write and rewrite. Take pleasure in seeing the pages accumulate.

Keep writing. Take control, but be willing to be uncertain. You don't have to understand exactly what you're doing or where you're heading. Be patient with yourself. We've been creating stories since the beginning of human time. We know how stories work. Trust the language. Trust the story. Trust yourself. Be influenced by all the writers you've ever loved. Be influenced by music, birdsong, food, whatever else you've hated or loved. Writing is an act of exploration and discovery. This is your story. Honour it and give it time. Take risks. Write for longer than you think you can. Work hard. Wrestle with the story when you need to.

Use willpower. Make massive changes. Make nitpicking changes. Wait for those moments of grace when the writer disappears and the story seems to write itself. Those moments will come.

Love language. Read your work aloud. Feel it on your tongue and breath. Sing your sentences. Love the look of words, the shapes of paragraphs and pages. Love full stops and commas. Love the space around the words.

Accept self-doubt. That'll never go away. Be brave. Be dogged. Yes, groan and know that you're maybe the worst writer who has ever lived, but aim high and try to write as well as Shakespeare. Why not? Don't tell yourself too soon what kind of writer you are. Write hard, but be in the world as well. Live your life. Experiment with yourself. Surprise yourself by what you come to write. And accept rejection. It'll come your way. Snarl, spit, shrug and crack on. You'll show 'em, won't you? Yes, you will.

THINK OF HARALD
Andy Riley

I'm hoping other people in this book will handle big important points like 'give yourself permission to write utter crap', 'finish the first draft before you fiddle with the beginning', 'writing is rewriting' and 'don't be an arsehole'. These are all true, and vital, but there's something else we need to cover.

I utterly reject advice like 'the art of writing is the art of applying the seat of the pants to the seat of the chair'. It's dangerous, and not in a good way. The human body is designed for varied hunter-gatherer work: a bit of climbing, a bit of carrying, a bit of running, a lot of walking. It's not designed for a lifetime typing at a desk and chair. That can catch up with you and fuck you up. I take a holistic view of the job – you write with your mind, and with your body. If you think the state of your body doesn't matter much, you'll change your mind if you have a bout of crippling RSI and it feels like you've got a meat skewer in your forearm. That happened to me after nearly two decades as a writer and cartoonist. I got out of it, but it took a few years.

At minimum, you should swim, or do weights, or Pilates, or yoga, or whatever works for you. Running isn't enough. You need to be working your back and shoulders too. See a good physio before you get a problem. Show them how you sit and use a keyboard. Find out which muscles you're hammering too hard, and which ones you're barely working at all. Some predictions, if you're a writer: your pectorals are way too tight, your rhomboids are weak and your core could use some work. Learn trigger point massage. The best book to get is *The Trigger Point Therapy Workbook* by Clair Davies.

Don't use a mouse. Watch people who do; their forearm, poised between clicks, is in a state of perpetual tension. Get a trackpad. If you're sitting for a long time, stand up and move around every half an hour. Better yet, don't sit so much in the first place. Not just standing desks; I also make extensive use of a giant noticeboard. My ideas stage and my plotting stage are all done with a swarm of index cards on the wall. I'm up and pacing about.

My greatest discovery as a writer in the last ten years is the dictation feature on the iPhone. Go to: settings>general>keyboard>enable dictation. Now, when the keyboard pops up, there's a little microphone symbol next to the spacebar. Press it and speak. Siri will instantly transcribe everything you say. All my first drafts are dictated like this and I can't tell you how freeing it is. I leave the house and walk for hours, speaking the story into my phone. By the end of the day I'm far into the countryside, and I've got anything up to 4,000 words in a notes file which I email to myself. If I do it enough times, I have a book. Second draft onward, I'm much more deskbound – but for that exhilarating splurge draft, I'm plunging through woods and bounding over hills. I'm hunting and gathering the stories.

One of my writing heroes is Harald Hardrada, the Viking warlord who invaded England in 1066. He was ambushed by a bigger Anglo-Saxon army at Stamford Bridge. According to Snorri Sturluson, knowing he wouldn't live out the day, Harald dictated a poem, which has come down to us. Then he decided it was a crap poem, so he dictated a much better one, which also survives. And all while facing a thousand axe-wielding Anglo-Saxon maniacs. Now that's a proper writer, right there, and not a chair in sight.

GOLDEN RULES I

1. When mapping out your new book, an idea will often come to you when you least expect it. At the time you might think, oh, that's good, I must remember it. You probably won't. So, try to jot it down somewhere. I carry around a thick little notepad (my 'Writer's Block' – ho, ho, ho) or I use a dictation app on my iPhone.

2. Very early on, come up with the outline of what you plan to cover in your book, whether it's scribbled on a sheet of paper, Post-it notes on a wall or a list of bullet points in a Word file. Get that skeleton structure in place.

3. Find your writing space – somewhere you can feel comfortable for long stretches of time. I know this sounds like really obvious advice, but it's crucial. It's also more important to some people than others. For example, I'm lucky that I'm able to write in lots of different places: my study, my back garden, on the train on my daily commute ... Basically, if where you sit down to write *doesn't* allow you to escape into your inner universe and block out all external stimuli, then find somewhere else.

4. Don't worry if nothing happens as soon as you sit at your keyboard. If I have designated a writing day, then I will devote nine or ten hours to it, and I need a good hour just to get 'into the zone'.

5. Don't feel you need to exhaust all background research before you get going on the writing. If you're itching to start putting words down, do it. There will certainly be times when you *don't* feel like writing, so take advantage of those occasions when you are in the mood.

6. Don't feel you need to produce the final, polished version of a piece or chapter on the first or even second attempt. Get your ideas down first. Writing is like sculpting – you chisel away at your block of marble to get the basic shape, then you spend far longer carving, refining and honing it.

7. When you think you have your prose ready, try reading it out aloud (TO YOURSELF). You will be far more likely to pick up any mistakes, clunky wording or repetitions than if you just read it silently.

8. Don't feel that anything you've written is sacrosanct, even if you've spent a long time crafting it. You might come to it afresh and, at a whim, feel that a paragraph or even an entire section has to go. Do it.

9. More accomplished writers than me might baulk at this next piece of advice ... but I do love to use a thesaurus. Often, the word I am looking for is hiding from me, just below the surface of my consciousness. So I pick a word as close as I can to it, then I go to a thesaurus. The word I want may not be on the list of synonyms, but there will likely be another word there that is closer to the one I'm looking for. So, I try again with this new word. Nine times out of ten, I'll eventually find just what I'm looking for.

10. Write 'in your own voice'. Don't try to be someone else. Often, I read the work of others and think, wow, that's so eloquent, insightful, poetic, funny, and so on – I wish I'd written it, or, there's no way I could have put it so well. But then I tell myself that maybe I have other strengths. My writing style is unique to me and I should not worry that there are so many authors out there who are more talented wordsmiths.

Sophie Anderson

1. *There are stories inside all of us.* We're made of them. We've been fed them since we were babies. We've heard them, read them and watched them dance around us. They swirl in our souls. If we open ourselves up and stand out of their way, they flow from us as something new and beautiful and unique.

2. *Trust your story.* Give your story time and space to grow and explore. Let it wander and experiment and get things wrong. Let it be daft and silly and deep and serious. Let it be pragmatic and soulful. Let it sit and stew. Let it fall apart and pull itself together again. Eventually, it will become the story it needs to be. Because stories know what they are.

3. *Feed your story.* Stories need nourishment. They like beauty and fresh air and conversation. They like books, folktales and legends; theatres, cinemas and museums; art and music. And they need *love*. Stories are vulnerable things. To grow into themselves, they need encouragement and love.

4. *Give your story immediate attention.* If a story is itching inside you, now is the time to write it. Don't wait for a new notebook, or a nice, quiet writing space, or for the children to start school, or leave home. Write NOW. Write HERE. On the inside of a cereal box in the kitchen surrounded by mess and noise if you have to. Just write, in all the moments you can.

5. *Let your story bring joy into your life.* Play with its words, its sentences and structure, its rhyme and rhythm and the cadence of its voice. Play with its punctuation. Speak it. ♪ Sing it ♪. Decorate it, doodle around it. Ride the rollercoaster of its bumpy paragraphs,

and swim through its smooth chapters. See what your story teaches you. See where it takes you. And smile.

6. *Let your story be emotional.* Write with your heart and soul. Laugh, cry, sob with despair, growl in anger, tingle with anticipation, quake in fear, recoil in disgust, swell and soar with happiness. Write *with* feeling. Write *to feel* something. Write to release your feelings, to understand them. Pour your emotions into your story, lay them bare upon the page. Look at them, see how they give your story life.

7. *Never be ashamed of your story.* With stories, there is no right or wrong. Let your story be what it is. If it finds its way into the wider world, some people will like it, and some will not. And that's fine. Don't write thinking about how others will judge your story. Write for yourself. Write without fear ... *But be respectful.* If you don't know what cultural appropriation is, find out. Don't misinform. Don't perpetuate stereotypes. Do your research. Talk to people. Listen to them. Think.

8. *Don't lose yourself in a story.* Come up for air. Look at the stars and the sea, the raindrops and the puddles. Don't forget the people you love. Because they are the real story.

9. *When a story drains your creativity, refill the well.* Stories are greedy. They will take and take and take, and leave you feeling empty. But they can never take it all. There will always be an ember of creativity left. And you can fan this back to life with a simple breath, a walk in a park, a swim in a lake. Don't panic when your creative energies fade. It's a natural cycle, and with a little encouragement they will return.

10. *When it's time to edit your story, be bold, be brave.* For a story to become the best it can be, it will need editing. And this may hurt. It may involve deleting beautiful words and well-structured sentences, poetic paragraphs and charming chapters. Maybe even whole characters who feel like old friends. They aren't necessarily bad or wrong. Perhaps they are in the wrong place at the wrong time. Perhaps they were scaffolding for the story – vital at the time of construction, but not needed any more. It can be hard to say goodbye, but for your story to fly it must shake off those downy feathers.

11. *Let your story surprise you.* Lay a place at the table for an unexpected guest. Embrace the unforecasted storm. Allow kind characters to do something cruel. Let the selfish ones sacrifice themselves for the greater good. Be surprised. Be amazed. And if you set out to write ten tips on working with stories, let them be eleven.

Philip Ardagh

1. *Never lose sight of the joy.* Once, I used to write for the sheer pleasure and excitement of it. For the joy. I wrote on scraps of paper, in old diaries and exercise books because I had words and phrases, ideas and stories fighting to get out. I remember a childhood holiday with my parents in Cornwall, lying on a beach, screwing up my eyes against the sun, and writing. I remember the smell of sun-warmed Biro-ink and paper. For twenty-eight years now, I've earned my living as a writer and, for around twenty-five of these, it's been my sole source of income. There are deadlines, pressures and expectations to live up to so it's not the same – it can never be quite the same – but I've never forgotten that, for me, it's the best job in the world.

2. *Never take things for granted.* I've never had a plan, but the books I've written have taken me around the world: Australia, China, Europe, the UAE, Singapore, India and the USA and Canada. I've stayed in amazing hotels, eaten wonderful meals and met some fascinating people. At one stage, I visited North America three years in a row, all because of the stories that began life as ideas in my head. I've been spoilt with hotel suites and five-star treatment, but that doesn't mean I don't expect – and won't accept – a tiny room in a B&B for a small festival somewhere in the UK. An author's life is one of extreme contrasts. Live it and learn to love it, but never think it's your RIGHT. One day, it'll all be over, anyway.

3. *Never lose that childish glee.* If, for some unknown reason, you find yourself staying in a room with a bath with more valves and levers than a submarine; if you land yourself the most amazing deal with your favourite publisher; if you connect with an editor who totally gets you; if you find yourself next to an author or actor or film star you adore – and writers do get to mix with the strangest assortment of folk – ENJOY it. Let it soak in and relish it. I've collaborated with

Paul McCartney, though I'm as musical as a Weetabix. I was sent to Lapland to train to be one of Father Christmas's elves, although I'm 6 ft 7 in. tall. These were FUN TIMES. Gleeful times. Shout it from the rooftops if you can't literally bounce on the beds.

4. *Make routine routine.* I'm not one of those writers who gets up at 10 a.m., ensures that I write at least three whole sentences by midday then get out of my silk pyjamas, shower, have my first mint julep of the day, followed by the afternoon to myself. I'm generally at my laptop from 9.00 or 10.00 to 5.30, with an hour off for lunch and Netflix, and am often typing away again in the evening, once my son has gone to bed. If I do nip into town to do something, I feel like I'm playing truant from school. It feels wrong. And it works for me. If I'm not actually writing, I'm generating invoices or doing admin. I don't have an agent, so everything's down to me.

5. *Use social media to be social.* People see me when I'm out and about because when I'm *not* out and about they won't see me. This gives a false impression of my varied and glamorous – so-not-true – lifestyle. I spend the majority of my time at home working but, because I attend launches and parties and award ceremonies and book festivals, there's this idea that I'm forever out there. Because I'm at home most of the time and don't have much of a social life outside work, I maintain most of my friendships online. I've made what I feel are genuine connections and friendships that way. My online persona is my 'public' persona, if you like. I don't post messages or photos relating to my family on Facebook, Twitter or Instagram ... but that's not to say that plenty of it isn't fun or silly or, sometimes, very rude. My online voice is very much my authorial voice. I advise against using the medium simply to plug your latest book or project. People soon tire of it. Be yourself but make them want to stay for the show.

6. *Be respectful but don't be afraid.* To me, publishers are partners. I don't work for them. If they're right for me and I'm right for them, we're in it together. I've never had an agent so I get up close and personal. Authors are at the heart of publishing. We create the product. (There's that dreaded word, but publishing is a business.) We're the ones who write the words that put the images in people's heads. We make what the customer is buying. And that's a strong position to be in and something not to lose sight of. I count many editors, marketing and PR folk as my friends, but they can jump ship tomorrow. I can only ever be, and represent, me.

7. *Surround yourself with nice stuff.* Nice as in meaningful, not expensive! Illustrators often have studios away from home, or in outhouses at the bottom of their garden. Authors are more inclined to have a room in their house, with many notable exceptions. Illustrators' studios always seem to be filled with interesting things, from animal skulls and carousel horses to plastic figurines and brightly coloured toys. We authors can take a leaf out of their book. My study contains outsized pocket watches, knitted cakes on a stand, stone eggs, unusual bookends supporting many books, magnifying glasses, cuddly owls ... I think I've said too much already. This is the room where I spend much of my life, so I want to make it ME.

8. *Remember that your success depends entirely on the failure of others.* No it doesn't. Most writers' lives have ups and downs. I'm lucky in that I've had more ups than downs – so far – but an author who's up there and always stays up there is an unusual creature. In the course of your career you'll meet authors whose books bring untold joy to the masses but leave you scratching your head, mumbling, 'But WHY?' You'll think, 'It should have been me!' It's human nature. Even Mother Teresa was no Mother Teresa. She said she did what she did because she believed God had told her to. Not

out of compassion. If He'd said, 'Go fishing!', her life might have taken a very different turn. But you can get used to the vagaries of publishing: liking people whose books you hate and, more sadly, disliking people whose books you love ... but little if any of it has to do with your own success and failure. Live for the words.

9. *Don't buy a dog.* The majority of authors and illustrators I know either have dogs or crave one. Dogs make great companions. They're excellent subjects for photographs and online posts. They're inspiration for books. They're there for you when you're feeling unloved and alone in the house after a bad day's writing. They give you a reason to get outside and enjoy the fresh air; an excuse to get exercise. Dog-walking can keep you fit. Writing is a very sedentary experience. I live opposite a wood. The trees in my front garden touch the trees in the wood in a canopy above the lane that divides the two. I'm writing this halfway through 2019 and do you know how many morning or lunchtime walks I've had so far this year? Exactly none. I hate exercise. A dog would get me fit. Don't buy a dog. Stay at your desk. Work.

10. *Be kind.* You'll find that life is kinder back. And we could all do with a bit of kindness right now.

Yaba Badoe

1. One of the best pieces of advice I've received from an editor, an old friend who was instrumental in helping me get my first novel published, was: 'Writing is hard work. It doesn't pay much and it takes a lot of time. So, unless you feel you really can't live without writing, don't.'

2. Write stories you haven't yet read, which you'd love to discover. Growing up as a child of African heritage in England in the 1960s and 1970s, I never saw my experience reflected in the books I devoured. I think it was this desire to see myself in fairy stories, Greek myths, Enid Blyton and psychological thrillers that encouraged me to tell my own stories.

3. Writing requires time, space, money and discipline. I'm fortunate enough to have a home with a study. Even so, I've spent most of my working life juggling making films for television with writing in my spare time. If I'm in Ghana I get up very early to write as much as I can before noon, when the sun is at its hottest. Wherever I am in the world I try to write for three hours uninterrupted every weekday. For those hours I use an app, Cold Turkey, to keep me away from distractions online.

4. I admire writers who are able to start with a clear outline of the story they intend to tell. I usually have a sense of the beginning of a story and its end. Somehow I have to find my way from start to finish by listening closely to my characters and allowing them to help me shape their narrative.

5. I keep a notebook for every novel I work on. If I get stuck I use it as a diary to help me unravel dilemmas I'm having with characters and plot. I'll jot ideas down, try out dialogue, elaborate on images that

have caught my imagination, and write down snippets of conversation I've overheard that may suit one of my characters. In short, anything that tickles my fancy that relates to what I'm focused on goes in my notebook.

6. I find writing the first draft of a story takes the most time and effort. I read my paragraphs out loud to appreciate the music and rhythm of the words I'm using. If something's off key, I'll hear it and hone it until it works.

7. I can become so absorbed in what I'm writing that I stay glued to my screen for hours. Remember to get up from time to time to move around. Movement not only gets your blood flowing again but also unlocks ideas. Best of all, exercise regularly, especially if you're stuck.

8. An editor you trust is worth her weight in gold. A rule of thumb when I hadn't yet found a publisher was that if two people in my writing community made the same comment, I had to listen carefully and make changes.

9. Nothing surpasses the rush of a good story as it tumbles out. So much so, that no matter how difficult and frustrating writing can be at times, being swallowed by a whale is among the most magical, satisfying experiences of my life.

Alex Bell

1. *Be curious about the world.* You might be lucky and get a bolt of inspiration out of the blue, but usually ideas come when you're in the middle of learning something, doing a cool new thing or seeing a part of the world for the first time. So go on as many adventures as you can.

2. *Empathize.* A large part of being a novelist is putting yourself in other people's shoes and trying to see things from their point of view. So being able to empathize with others who may be very different from you is a wonderful skill to cultivate.

3. *Persistence is key.* I've had stories rejected many times and I know this will happen again too. Sometimes a book isn't quite the right book, or it's not the right time. And that can be demoralizing. But you have to pick yourself back up, move on to the next project and try again. You can't ever win if you're not in the race. It's as simple as that.

4. *Listen to feedback.* It can be hard receiving feedback, but it can also really improve your writing to get an outsider's perspective. Listen carefully to any comments, implement the changes you think will improve the book, but don't be afraid to stick to your guns if you disagree either. It's your story.

5. *Have a Siamese cat (or two).* Perhaps this one is just me, but my two Siamese are pretty indispensable to the process. They keep me company while I write and frequently demand I take several mini-breaks throughout the day to cater to their whims.

6. *Surround yourself with people who support your writing.* Writing can feel lonely at times, but having family members cheering you on from the sidelines makes all the difference.

7. *Take time to read.* Writers are readers first, after all, and falling in love with the wonderful novels written by other people can help fuel your own passion.

8. *Don't compare.* Admire other writers' novels by all means, but don't get sucked into the comparison trap. Let them do their thing, and you do yours.

9. *Write the book you most want to read.* It's good to be aware of the market, but there's no use chasing trends. They change too rapidly and are unpredictable. Write the book you most want to read yourself.

10. *Believe in the magic of storytelling.* Ultimately, most of us would make more money if we committed the same hours to almost anything else. So don't write for fame and fortune. Write because you believe in the magic of stories to entertain, to make people feel less alone and to open doorways to extraordinary adventures we would never have experienced otherwise.

Edward Carey

1. *There are no rules in fiction.* I think that's wonderful. And what a relief. Those that give you strict rules about writing dos and don'ts are telling you lies. But also: each short story or novel has its own set of rules and you'll have to work out what they are as you go along.

2. *Read.* Read, read, read, read, read, read, read, read. Don't ever stop reading other people's work. Read. READ! Keep your mind open for inspiration everywhere, but most of all read and read and read. I love the story about Márquez reading Kafka's *Metamorphosis* and suddenly feeling liberated by it. He hadn't realized writing could be like that. Kafka's imagination gave him permission to leap further, to push his writing. Which brings me to ...

3. *Dare yourself!* Push yourself as far as you can, ask yourself have I really written that as well as I can, have I fully imagined it? Listen out for the little voice in your head that says 'Yes, that'll do', and respond 'No, no it won't do yet.'

4. *Write about what you care about.* Not what you think others might be interested in. It may be stamps, or elephant seals or candy-cane chimneys. It doesn't matter as long as you're passionate.

5. *Don't be afraid to fail.* Don't keep wondering – will this be published, is this good enough? The best space for a piece of writing to exist in is in a state of experiment, where if it works that's great but if it fails that's fine too. A certain lightness to allow the thing to be itself is really important – and not always easy. But the point is, the writing is being done for the love of writing, not for anything else. Writing it – be it comedy or tragedy – should be enjoyable, you're not writing to punish yourself. I don't believe in the flatulence of people who say how hard it is to be a writer and the agony of

the writer's existence. Who chose to be a writer anyway? Frankly, you're writing by choice not at gunpoint, and also it's a pleasure.

6. *Keep it to yourself.* If you're working on a long project, probably even a short one, don't talk about it, keep it quiet. Let it grow on its own terms. I'm not much for the #amwriting Twitter noise, far better I think to let a thing grow quietly on its own, for it just to be the writer and the growing project. Each time you talk about a novel before it's fully formed, it dies a little. When a good draft is done, when you've gone as far as you think you can on your own, that's the time to give it to other trusted eyes.

7. *Maps.* It has always helped me to draw maps of the places my characters inhabit and also to make quick drawings of the characters themselves. This is not about creating works of art, it doesn't matter how artful these drawings are, it's about knowing your world (whether fantastical or realistic) and stopping your characters from being little more than floating heads.

8. *Put it away.* Once you've got a draft of something, and made it the best you think it can be, then leave it alone. Put it in a desk drawer for a few months, don't look at it, try not to even think about it, and then, at last, take it out once more. Now you'll see it clearer than ever before. You'll be reading it almost as if you hadn't written it yourself – and that's ideal. Now you'll be able to see mistakes and be much clearer where to go with the piece. (One novel I wrote took me fifteen years to finish and I could only complete it after I'd convinced myself I'd absolutely abandoned it, then, later, when I recalled it once more I saw at last how to finish it.)

9. *Discipline.* This may sound very gloomy and uninspired, but the most essential thing about writing is being disciplined. If you're not willing to work extremely hard and put very many hours in, then forget it. (You don't have to write every day, but if you're working on a novel, for example, that routine is certainly very helpful.) Keep a notebook with you.

10. *Be the strangest version of yourself.*

Frank Cottrell-Boyce

1. Writing something good is not about technique – it's not about story structure or the great adverb conspiracy or show-not-tell – it's all about character. Your own character. It's about keeping going and keeping faith. Keeping going when it's all falling apart. Keeping going when no one else is interested. Keeping going when it's no fun, when it feels less like composition and more like a self-inflicted migraine. Keeping faith that at some point some unexpected electrical charge will pull everything together and it will feel like the day you first learnt to ride a bike. Above all it is about remembering that that day will only come if you keep turning up and grinding it out, and that the best ideas do not come while you're thinking or planning but while you are writing. Sometimes they don't come till just after you've pressed 'send'. But they do come.

2. That being the case, do all you can to mitigate the misery. For me this means writing my first draft in pen in a notebook (I photograph the pages so I don't lose them). This means I'm not locked into some kind of terrible mental fight with the temptation to go on Twitter or mainline some kind of newsfeed or 'just look up' something on Wikipedia. Look it up afterwards! It also means setting a target for the day. Not a macho target – something to aim for. A target that is some kind of agreement with yourself about what represents a decent day's work. That way you don't wake up every morning thinking I have to finish my novel today. And you don't go to bed that night with a crushing sense of failure. And you can walk away from your desk with an easy conscience, thinking, that was a good day's work.

3. All that stuff about story structure, adverbs and show-not-tell that I said didn't matter while you're writing your first draft – they are absolutely all that matters once you start rewriting.

Cressida Cowell

1. Make up your own rules. I love reading books like Stephen King's *On Writing*, but I have no intention of following his or anyone else's rules. Similarly, I love reading Hemingway, but when I write myself I stick in endless adverbs and twiddly, unnecessary bits of language because I *like* twiddly, unnecessary bits of language. The following rules are all my own, and you don't have to follow them ...

2. Read a lot. I try to read as much as I possibly can because it gives me a feel for the way that stories can be written.

3. DO NOT BORE THE CHILD READER. I've put that one in capitals because it is so important. There are so many other things the child reader could be doing with their time. They could, for instance, be staring at those lovely little machines that are increasingly taking over their lives. So I don't want to bore them, for goodness' sake. Statistics on kids reading for pleasure suggest they are doing less and less of it, so I feel I have to work like a demon to make sure they want to keep reading.

4. DO NOT BORE THE ADULT WHO IS HOPEFULLY READING OR LISTENING TO THE BOOK WITH THE CHILD. Rainbow fairy books are great at getting children reading, but frankly they're on their own with those ones.

5. Never underestimate the child reader. Children's attention span is much shorter nowadays, and they have become more visual, but they haven't become less intelligent.

6. DO NOT LOOK TO LEFT OR RIGHT. Who cares how or what everyone else is doing? Seriously, if I worried about that, I would drive myself crazy. I care about what *I'm* doing.

7. Create a protagonist who people care about. If they don't care about the protagonist, it doesn't really matter what you do with them, you can throw them off cliffs and put them in the most fiendishly brilliant plot situation, but who cares? You don't want to read on if you don't care what happens to the person it's happening to.

8. WRITE. This seems obvious, but I try and get in the writing shed by at least 8.30 a.m. and write for as long as possible.

9. Engage with some of the 'rules' of the industry, e.g. 'Meet the Deadline'. If the Sales department think a proof might be helpful in selling book rights in Bologna, I do try to make whatever deadline there is for achieving that. Even if I drive my family and myself crazy and I only just squeak it in at the last minute. That goes, unfortunately, for all deadlines. Douglas Adams said something very funny about them whizzing by, but I've always found it a better idea to meet them. Whenever I find the above rule about deadlines a little taxing, I remind myself that Shakespeare wrote two really rather good plays a year while dodging the plague/moving the playhouse/ rehearsing/acting/managing the company/laughing at Armin the clown's poor jokes and massaging the leading actor's ego. I know he was a genius, but STILL.

10. Move yourself when writing. I try to write books that make me laugh, and cry, and be scared, and think. I try to write books that have a little wisdom in them, without being preach-y. If the story doesn't move ME, how will it move the reader?

Inua Ellams

1. We begin writing when we see a way the world is, or could be. This particular eye is a writer's most precious possession. It evolves from our concerns, memories, misunderstandings and motivations. Guard it well. Don't let it get infected by how others see the world.

2. Always have something on you with which to capture ideas ... a notebook, a Dictaphone, a napkin. Inspiration doesn't announce its arrival and doesn't wait to leave.

3. Gather a scrapbook of paragraphs, poems, scenes, essays, short stories etc., that remind you of how great and limitless literature can be. When I get lost, I go back to re-read them. They centre and power me to go forth and create.

4. Before you begin to write, all words, all their infinite arrangements, all the limitless possibilities of creation gather behind your pen, as if a god, soon to utter into an empty galaxy 'Let There Be Light'. Writing is that blasphemous, that holy. Be careful.

5. When you finish writing, if it doesn't work, throw it away. There are other infinite arrangements and limitless possibilities gathered behind your pen. All you have done is scratched one down. Scratch again. Writing is that pedestrian, that common. Be careless.

6. To quote the great singer and songwriter Lauryn Hill, 'Everything you did has already been done.' Don't pressure yourself trying to be groundbreaking or original. It is impossible and ultimately pointless. All you should be trying to be, is you.

7. In early hip hop culture, ingenuity came from sampling – mixing odd bits of records with other bits of records until they became new

songs. So it is with writing. Mix odd bits of yourself with odder bits of yourself. The smoother the mix, the clearer your voice. This is you becoming you.

8. To quote Lauryn Hill again: 'It could all be so simple, but you'd rather make it hard.' Above all, whatever it is you are writing, strive for simplicity. Achieving this is hard enough.

9. Stories are told for many reasons, in many parts of the world and in many different ways: for social change, for political activism, as a form of witness, worship, remembrance, as entertainment, as propaganda, to dazzle, to confuse, to illustrate, to deny, to highlight, to beautify. Make sure the reason you are writing what you are writing is fixed and clear in your mind. When you get lost, stunned by how many choices you have to make, as you always will, this will help you out.

10. Remember to have fun.

Maz Evans

For a creative, I am curiously inept at creation. Indeed, my only successful creations – if the defining criterion for success is that they survived the process – are my books and my babies. The creative journeys for both endeavours have much in common, so my advice for bringing either creation into the world is essentially the same.

1. *It's going to hurt.* There is no escaping this fundamental truth and you have a right to full disclosure. Once this creation is inside you, it needs to come out and no one's contrived a painless way to do it. Expect to sit uncomfortably at times.

2. *You can't force it to grow.* Your creation has a life of its own. You can't compel it to do anything before it's ready. Cultivate the right environment for it to develop – then let time do its thing. It'll be on its feet in its own time. Then it won't leave you alone.

3. *Spend more time with it than posting about it.* It's easy to spend so much time broadcasting your creation that you're not actually paying it enough attention. Also – whispered with love – *no one's actually as interested in it as you are …*

4. *Show it love every day.* There are no shortcuts – you have to put in the hours for your creation to flourish. Even when you'd rather undergo root canal treatment from a dipsomaniac donkey, you have no choice but to show up and tend it. But do consider an appropriate analgesic.

5. *Some days just suck.* There will be times when no matter what you do, you cannot get it right. They are a painful, but necessary, part of the process. Get through them, try to learn from them and always move past them. But above all, expect them.

6. *Look after yourself.* Your creation can be all-consuming, but you must make time to tend to your needs too. Meditate, ruminate, vegetate – whatever you need to stay well. Because this thing can't thrive without you. And nor can you.

7. *Don't compare yours to everyone else's.* That person's is bigger than yours. That person has produced three in the time it's taken you to produce one. And everyone seems to love *that* person's more ... This way madness lies. Celebrate the one you made. You're heroic for doing it. And frankly, you're stuck with yours anyway.

8. *The first one gets the most attention.* Harsh, but true. You did it! You created something wonderful! Everyone was so excited the first time! And they're super happy you're doing it again ... just don't expect as many presents.

9. *The same recipe creates very different dishes.* You think you've figured it all out – what works, what doesn't, how to do this thing right ... and then another one comes along and you realize you haven't got a clue. Each creation is unique. So will your relationship with it be.

10. *Enjoy and endure – nothing lasts.* You are on an extraordinary voyage with many zeniths and nadirs. Be they sleeplessness, euphoria, worry, success – all these things shall pass. Treat these many imposters just the same. And always, always keep a bottle handy – just in case.

Lev Grossman

Like a lot of writers, I'm sometimes visited by the ecstatic feeling that I finally and totally understand how to write, and that I will never write badly again. *Weave a circle round him thrice*, etc. This revelation usually arrives about five minutes after I've had my first coffee.

It never lasts, of course. But while I'm in the grip of it I often try to write down, in a pithy sentence or two, whatever great truth about writing it is that I think I've grasped. Sometimes it's impossible to decipher later what the hell it was I was trying to say, but I keep the more coherent ones in a file on my desktop and refer to them when I'm feeling lost, which is most of the time.

I've reproduced a few of them below. I apologize for the slightly bullying tone – it's myself I'm trying to bully, not you. Also keep in mind that the originals were written in **bold**, ALL CAPS, each one followed by six or seven exclamation marks!!!!!!! Feel free to mentally restore the punctuation and formatting if that adds anything.

1. The problem in writing is control. Nothing is more formless and inchoate than a book that hasn't been written yet. There's no playing field, no guardrails, no frame, not even any physical laws to constrain you. There's nothing that will stop your book from veering completely off the road and/or completely falling apart. The thing that gives it form is the story. It's the story that will keep your book together and on the road. When it's all falling apart, go back to that.

2. The first draft is about figuring out how the characters feel about everything. The second draft is figuring out how they feel about their feelings. And so on and so on. Iterate until you approach something like the fractal complexity of what it's like to be alive.

3. From a cognitive point of view writing fiction is hard ... but it's not *that* hard. It's not playing chess with twenty people blindfolded. It's

not doing differential calculus in your head. You don't see a lot of novelists who abandoned careers in nuclear physics to write novels. My point is that you are smart enough to write your novel. If it feels like you're not – if it feels so complicated that it won't fit in your head, and you're thinking as hard as you can and you're still stuck – that probably means that you're thinking *too* hard. Try thinking less and feeling more. It's probably a feeling problem rather than a thinking problem. And there's a codicil to this, which is that if you do happen to be clever, if you can actually play chess with twenty people blindfolded, keep it to yourself. Nobody cares. All readers want is to feel.

4. Writing is what you say and how you say things, but also the order in which you say them. Don't always write linearly, like in an essay. Keep the rhythms of thought and speech choppy, the way they are in real life. The rhythms of consciousness are very broken and illogical, and you have to mimic them in prose. Mix up logical steps, separate cause and effect, play with paragraph breaks, whatever breaks up those monotonous regular beats.

5. When prose feels smart and polished it's usually the transitions. Paragraphs are the bricks, the transitions are the mortar. They show that you understand the logical connection between what you just said and what you're about to say. When you've finished a piece of writing it ought to be an unbroken chain of paragraphs and transitions, like a string of Christmas tree bulbs that all light up.

6. Remember how readers read: at great speed and with no regard for your feelings. You can spend three hours on a sentence, but the reader's still probably going to blow through it in about three seconds flat. Never forget that writing is slow, but reading is very very fast.

7. When you're stuck, write something terrible and fix it later. This isn't music, or dance, or stage acting. You don't have to get it right every day. Just get it right once, and it will be right forever.

8. You don't have to create tension. Tension is a naturally occurring phenomenon. People spend their whole lives in a state of tension. You're probably tense right now. So are your characters. Usually it's about finding that tension and bringing it to the surface.

9. When you're trying to decide between two things that might be motivating your character, and you find yourself thinking 'maybe it's both', it's definitely both.

10. Whenever you discover that you've made a rule, break the rule. If a story is predicated on the idea that one particular thing can never ever happen ... you have to make exactly that thing happen. There were two rules in *Twilight*, which were that Bella and Edward can never have sex, and Bella can never become a vampire. This is why we have *Breaking Dawn*.

11. There has never been an idea so good, or an inspiration so profound, that at some point in the process of writing it down it hasn't felt completely and utterly stupid. I would lay my life on the line that at some point during the composition of *Moby-Dick* Melville put his head in his hands and said: this is so damn stupid, Hawthorne's going to laugh his ass off.

Matt Haig

1. Do not write for the market. Write for you. Write for your best friend. Write for the ghost of Virginia Woolf. But don't write for the market because it's impossible to know what the market is. Create your own market. Differentiate or die.

2. The quickest way to write a bad novel is to be pretentious. Get your bullshit detector working early. Do not be Sean Penn. Do not say things to make them sound cleverer than they are. Clean the windows. Let readers know what is going on.

3. Try to be healthy. Hemingway said 'write drunk, edit sober'. I'd go even further. 'Write sober, edit sober.' Go for a run. Drink water. On writing days, be dull as hell and clear as crystal. The brain is a physical organ. Treat it as such.

4. Don't be scared of saying 'she said'. There is nothing worse than when you can feel the thesaurus groaning under the pressure. 'She stated/rejoined/declared.' These are all fine words but don't use them just to avoid 'said'. Said doesn't get in the way. Said disappears.

5. Really check that your autobiographical novel is going to interest people who haven't had your biography.

6. Describe love scenes emotionally, not anatomically. And as in life, handle genitals with care. And never compare them to anything. Similes have their place. But it's not in your underwear.

7. Back everything up. And email your document to yourself every day. This is the most important rule. The best novel you've ever written is the one you will leave in the back of an Uber.

8. Be brave. Novels have the space to explore things you can't explore elsewhere. That is their power. Don't be timid, go to the edge. Let characters feel the things they wouldn't talk about in real life. Don't be polite.

9. Ignore labels. Ignore 'literary' and 'commercial'. Write what you want to write without the worry of marketing definitions. There will always be a market for good stories. Just go for that.

10. Have fun. Do not bore yourself. Surprise yourself. Write like your life depends on it. Love writing and put that happy germ of love into it and that love will infect the reader and you will be happy and the reader will be happy.

Vashti Hardy

The *Brightstorm* adventures were inspired by one of my long-standing fascinations: the tales of real-life explorers and adventurers. During the writing of *Brightstorm* something struck me: as well as the core story of the twins, I had in some way also written a metaphor for the writing process – being an explorer and being a writer hold some fascinating parallels. So, my ten tips for surviving the writing life are reflections on how, in the pursuit of our art, we are also true explorers, albeit of a different landscape: that of the imagination.

1. *Imagination and vision.* To step into the unknown, to imagine what could be, to ask questions of our world and be curious, are tandem qualities of both explorers and writers. Push into the unknown, even if it makes you feel uneasy. That's where the richest discovery and learning can come from.

2. *Positivity and optimism.* When interviewing candidates for his Trans-Antarctic Expedition, it is said that Shackleton looked for character and temperament above seamanship; he valued cheerfulness and a sense of humour. In writing, positivity will see you through many situations and along the (often) rocky road of a writing life.

3. *Tenacity.* In *Brightstorm* the twins continually overcome barriers. Not letting the tough times debilitate you is key to progression.

4. *Valuing loyalty.* Explorers usually work with a crew, and your writing crew, whether critique partners, agents, editors, designers, illustrators, publicists, sales and, of course, readers, are all your crew and you are stronger together. Go find your best writing crew.

5. *Adaptability.* Explorations can be full of twists and turns, no matter how well planned; think of how Shackleton's *Endurance* became

unexpectedly trapped in ice. Be flexible and adaptable, embrace the editing process. Even if you are losing large portions of writing, nothing is ever lost in the learning process.

6. *Conviction.* Doubt can be debilitating. In exploration, making a well-informed and instinctive decision can be key to survival. Self-doubt can be communicated in your words, even if you don't realize it. Self-belief will shine through, but not the kind of self-belief that comes with an overblown ego, rather the reflective kind that comes from working hard, and from having something to say or discuss.

7. *Making tough decisions.* I paused submitting the book my agent signed me for, because we weren't sure it would be the best first novel. It was tough to step away and write something new, but I trusted my agent's advice and my gut feeling. *Brightstorm* was the result of the next year's work, which became my first published novel.

8. *Focus.* Explorers risk life or death based on their decisions. Writing may not be life or death, but focus can see you through the tough times. Remember that there are things you can control, and things you can't. Focus on creating the best story or the best art you possibly can, not on the things you can't control in publishing.

9. *Resilience.* Flexibility and the spirit to keep going through the ups and downs, to learn from the journey, will help you grow as a writer.

10. *The desire to pursue true North.* Every explorer must keep sight of their bearings, just as every writer is looking to find the right direction for the story they want to tell. As there are thousands of routes to explore, there are thousands of ways to tell a story. Don't be afraid to change direction if a better way presents itself.

PICTURING

BE A LABRADOR

Be kind. Avoid being critical g
yourself when you are doing
your best.

BE A MACAW

Be proud to show gf
what you've created.

BE A CAIMAN

Snatch moments g
creativity whenever
they appear.

BE A TORTOISE

Take your time deciding
how you spend your energy.

BE A HONEY BEE

Know your goals
and work hard.

BE A LION

Be brave and
take risks.

BE A BOTTLENOSE
DOLPHIN

Enjoy every part g the
creative process.

WRITE LIKE AN ANIMAL
Lorna Scobie

BE A CHEETAH
Be quick to react
to opportunity.

BE A FENNEC FOX
Be aware and observe
the world around you,
with all your senses.

BE A BLUE WHALE

Be calm, be steady, be persistent.
Keep swimming, even when it
seems like you are on your own —
you are not, and you can do it.

DRAW AND LOOK
Anthony Browne

I have always loved telling stories through pictures – I've kept some of my early childhood drawings and they all contain jokes, speech bubbles and snippets of descriptive writing. It wasn't until I was twenty-eight that I decided to try to make a career out of it. I love the combination of words and pictures, seeing the book take shape. Often the pictures can illustrate different aspects of the story that the words don't tell.

When I make a picture book it's nearly always loosely auto-biographical, so the illustrations often refer to my life and interests. When children ask me 'where do you get your ideas from?' I usually say from everywhere – my own childhood, things my children told me, stories I've read, films I've watched and paintings I've seen. Over a period of time I found that I was able to use images in the background to tell parts of the stories that weren't in the text – like clues to what is really going on in a character's emotional and mental state.

The words and pictures generally come together at the same time. At first I have an idea in my head, which is a bit like remembering a dream. Often several fragments of an idea stay latent in my head for some time before they mature, gradually coming together to form something more coherent and reachable. I then draw out a series of twenty-four rectangles (representing the twelve double-page spreads which form the main part of a typical picture book) and fill them with very rough drawings and scrawls of text. In my mind there is a kind of animation to the idea, and I view my storyboard almost exactly as a film-maker would. Rather than the fixed pictures they will eventually become, I view the boxes as frames or scenes from the story, with a clear sense of progression through time. 'Playing out' the book in this way ensures that the visual and the textual come to me at the same time.

Having made my storyboard, I cut out the individual 'frames' and stick them into a small book. The dummy is the first incarnation of the idea that I show to my editor. With the dummy as a reference, we discuss the general qualities of the prospective book. There is rarely criticism of the pictures at this stage, but suggestions are offered as to how I could improve the text, the layout and the general rhythm.

I go back to my studio and set to work on the final pictures, starting by making slightly more detailed preliminary drawings on thin layout paper, the proportions of which correspond with the final book. As they are drawings, I can afford to make mistakes at this point, and alter the image until I am satisfied with it. To make the final paintings just slicker versions of the preliminary drawings would dampen my interest, so I always leave plenty to improvise. I then trace the drawings on to watercolour paper and start work creating the final image.

I think it's important to read and write as much as possible. Write as much as you can from your own experience, taking influences from things that happened to you as a child, other people's stories, paintings, films, dreams – and your imagination. Many people don't seem to appreciate our amazing gift of sight. We spend much of life not noticing things, just look at a crowd of people walking through an art museum spending more time reading the captions than looking at the paintings. One way to encourage us to use our visual capacities is to draw. When we draw we *really look* at the world.

TO THE TEMPLE
Piers Torday

Once upon a time, a traveller had a dream.

They dreamt that they saw, arising out of the desert, a great temple. It was a new structure, yet had the solidity of considerable age, as if it had always been there. In the traveller's mind, the temple was dimly lit, candles flickering in the dark recesses, and every detail of the building was shrouded in shadow.

Despite this, everything about the vision betokened clarity to the traveller. They felt sure that if they could only reach and apprehend the temple, there would be a revelation. Upon arrival, there would be brightness, light, order and a deep, lasting satisfaction which would quench their thirst for understanding. For all eternity.

The next day, upon waking, the traveller resolved to set out for this temple. But with every hour of daylight that passed, the process seemed more hopeless. They did not even know what country this temple was in, never mind how to get there. Would the journey best be achieved on foot or on horseback, or would it require boarding a plane? The vast candle-lit edifice, which had seemed so real during sleep, receded further and further from their mind's eye until they began to wonder whether they had even dreamt it at all.

Despair and despondency settled upon the traveller. They picked up books and put them down in a listless fashion, and took inconsequential, meandering strolls in different directions. They lounged, and snacked, and dozed, cursed, and wept. And at the end of all that, the way to the temple seemed no nearer or clearer.

But the next night, the dream returned. There was the temple again, looming out of the cold desert. This time, however, the traveller noticed something different about the temple. On the corner of the grandly sculpted roof there was a bird. The creature's plumage was a striking colour, its call melodic and haunting. In the dream, the traveller called up to the bird, which responded by flying off with a reproachful cry.

The next morning, the temple receded from view once more, but the colour and call of the bird briefly remained vivid to the traveller. In the city library, they researched the bird, but could find nothing that corresponded to the details in their mind. However, they found various similar birds, and as the traveller noted down the relevant details – different habitats, mating habits, diets and so on – their mind began to wander. How might such a bird have found a way to a temple in the desert, and why?

Taking a break for coffee from their labours in the airy library cafe, the traveller found themselves musing about one such bird that lived in a city. *Perhaps*, that bird had followed a mate to the temple? Or a prey? Or had the bird been kidnapped by the shadowy masters of the temple unknown? Idly, the traveller began to sketch a map on the back of a paper napkin of the route the bird might have taken from its urban nest to the temple, and as they began to imagine the line, other problems and opportunities occurred. What if a rare bird collector had spotted the creature in a city park, and resolved to add it to his grand collection, or what if a young child in another country had been drawn from domestic safety by the call, and then when the bird disappeared during a visit from a world-famous zoo ...

The traveller found their pen racing over page after page, as if guided by some phantom hand. Time seemed to pass and freeze at the same time. When at last they looked up, it was dusk outside, and the lights in the library burned low. The reading rooms were slowly emptying out into the night. They read back over what they had written.

No. That was not it at all! Why on earth had they written a thousand words about the kidnap of a rare bird? The temple seemed further away than ever before, and was not even mentioned in the pages before them.

But the traveller knew from experience that there was only one way to go. Onwards. They glanced at the clock on the library wall. Perhaps if they followed this bird's journey for just a few more pages, the way to the temple would be revealed, and they would be a step closer at last to the palace of their dreams.

A BLANK SHEET
James Mayhew

I never imagined I would be a writer. I'm dyslexic and arty. The literary world scared me. Then, when I was at art school, I wrote my first book, as a means to an end. I wanted to be an illustrator, and I needed a story. It was inspired by a very real visit to London museums as a child, with my sister Kate and our grandmother. It also allowed me to indulge my love of art and artists. *Katie's Picture Show* was published in 1989, and suddenly, there I was – a writer.

Writing picture book texts is a particular skill, and not many writers are succinct enough to create a successful text for thirty-two pages. I've grown to have enormous respect for those who manage to create the ideal texts for illustrators. Texts that leave breathing space for an illustrator's vision, texts with ebb and flow, and with the necessary gaps, waiting to be filled. Every single word has to be weighed and measured. There is no room for anything superfluous.

Good writing isn't about showing off or satisfying an ego. It's about something much simpler than that. It's about telling a story. Some books are built around a clever idea, or concept, others imitate what has gone before. But for me, the very best books are an act of generosity – of sharing. I write about the things I care about, the things I want to share with children, things that matter to me.

Where do I start? There is no magic formula – and I don't think there should be. Every single book is different and each process is unique. Sometimes I start with words, sometimes with drawings. But one thing is for sure, I always start with a *blank* sheet of paper. So I wrote a little poem to my familiar friend, which is really how it all begins:

Ode to a blank sheet of paper

For hours long have I gazed at you,
Like a field of pure, untouched snow.
Favourite pens and sharp pencils,
Lined up neatly, ready to go.
I dare not make a mark on you,
That first, little, hesitant line,
Because you are already perfect,
Full of such promise – mine.

You glare at me, blankly, silent,
I could just walk away.
I try my best to ignore you,
In truth, I have nothing to say.
I know that there's plenty more paper,
Be brave, dare to make a mistake!
Only with that act of courage,
Will my imagination awake.

That first mark, that first little letter,
curling, shaping a thought.
Like footprints, across that snow.
Journeys, adventures are sought.
Experiments and scribbles and errors,
Here are words that squabble and fight.
Trying to assemble an order,
For a sentence that looks and feels right.

As ideas grow, you fade gently,
Characters live, and scenes flow.
Farewell my blank sheet of paper,
At last my pen knows where to go.
Time is lost or forgotten,
In memories, dreams, I run.
I don't really know where I'm headed,
What matters is: I've begun.

MATHEMATICAL
Harry Baker

A mathematical poet's approach ...

> Searching for patterns *tends* to distract me from how
>   daunting it is,
> It turns out there is a pattern *in* everything.
> While the *weight* can overwhelm us within what we
>   want to write,
> Sometime*s even* heavy moments have their light.
> Most times – *I x*plore the rules and have a play with it.
> It's only afterwards that I'll know *if I've* got away
>   with it.
> Surely we must keep pushing *if our* instinct is for
>   the new,
> Even the ear*th re-e*nters every day after the last is
>   through.
> Withou*t w*onder, well I wonder quite how far we
>   would have come.
> And while you wonder – before you know it – you're
>   *done.*

THE SHAPE OF STARS
Emma Yarlett

Many writers begin creating a book by making a map. That seems to me a pretty good place to start, mapping out a territory to give your characters room to roam. Try it. Take the pressure off yourself. Pick up a pen and fill the looming blank page instead with an island, or a street of houses, a curving river or a mountain range. Before you know it, a story will begin to write itself in your head, emerging as you make new lines. Many stories are born this way. They don't always come when you're attached to a keyboard.

I adore maps. It has become a bit of a problem in my house, resulting in an urgent cull. We have map shower curtains, map cushions, map artworks, map books. Weirdly, given my obsession with maps and career as an illustrator, I've never actually had a map published. Perhaps this might be because I hold them in such high esteem that in the past I shied away from trying to create my own for print. Now, I just can't stop drawing them.

It's funny how two people can remember the same passage of time in completely opposite ways. I thought I'd always loved maps, but when I ask her now my mum thinks otherwise. She sees it all very straight down the line. Did I like road maps? No, she says, and therefore, goes her way of thinking, I must have despised all maps.

But did I enjoy *reading* maps growing up? No. Well, no as in I didn't read maps in the way most people read them: for directions, for *real* information. Perhaps this has something to do with my complete lack of any sense of direction. I'm also a little bit dyslexic. These paper things of beauty held hidden secrets that I could never quite understand. I'm sometimes asked by my young readers what my favourite colour is and my honest answer has always been 'rainbow'. Pictorially, I've always found maps enticing: the subtle shading, natural contours, overrun with grids and intricate, serifed typography. All the elements together become a thing of beauty. Yes, *even* the road maps.

I'm a very visual person. Often when I'm wandering around I'm not looking at the things in front of me, but rather creating imaginary worlds, places, characters and concepts in my brain – sifting through thoughts and images that might form a story. Many other writers work this way: walking and thinking, dreaming and writing nowhere near a computer at first. That comes much later in the edit once a draft is down.

Travelling to obscure places in my head and exploring made-up lands is something I do every day. When I think of my childhood as a reader my thoughts flicker straight to *Peter Pan*, but this must surely have been a Neverland from the Disney cartoon. Looking back again I was sure that Allan Ahlberg's *The Jolly Postman* was filled with maps, but I've just found a copy and it doesn't have any. I have a vague recollection of enjoying the physicality of that book so much as a child that I made my own map to pinpoint the postman's journey.

Though an imaginative streak definitely has its negatives it also brings a multitude of positives. Particularly so when a curious nature is paired with a love of words. I look at the world slightly askew. My dad is a space nerd and this meant that I spent long evenings as a kid with my eye glued to a telescope looking at the night sky, the craters of the moon and generally just getting lost in the inky depths. However, where he traced Taurus, Cetus or Orion, I found a farmhouse, a ray-gun and a rather lanky worm. Although not *technically* wrong, these weren't the shapes I was supposed to tick off the list, yet my dad encouraged me to see the way I wanted to see. Funnily enough, I've since written a book about a little boy who befriends the night sky and it's called *Orion and the Dark*. 'Lanky Worm and the Dark' didn't have quite the same ring.

But who determines what formations the stars make? Who orders the things we should or shouldn't see, or what imaginative journeys we go on when writing or drawing? Who gets to decide the shape of the stories the stars might tell? Surely our own personal imaginary maps are just as *real* as the real ones, and perhaps even more so. My mum may yet find one of my first maps, among a pile of early drawings and writings in the attic, and her memory of things might change. The shape of my story might change too and that's OK. When we narrate our lives, details reform all the time. Looking up again at the sky tonight, a lanky worm still feels far more real to me than all manner of Latin names.

NAIVETY IS GOOD
Helen Stephens

All the Secrets Nobody Told You About Writing and Illustrating a Picture Book ...

1. *Catch yourself out.* Write and sketch out your picture book on your bed, or somewhere that doesn't feel like a workspace. Pretend you will never show anybody what you're writing.

2. *Words and pictures.* The writing and drawing of a picture book form a simultaneous endeavour. Make thumbnail sketches with words alongside. You might not need all of the words if the pictures say it better.

3. *Make a dummy book.* Make a maquette of your picture book, see how the pacing works. Are you holding back surprises for page turns, does the story have light and dark spreads, are you using a good mix of double-page spreads and vignettes?

4. *Invest your royalties wisely.* In new thermals. It gets cold putting in the hours at your desk.

5. *Blow away the cobwebs.* Take the dog for long walks, it helps unblock tricky writing or illustrating problems.

6. *Play.* Once you are published and deadlines loom, it is easy to think that taking time out to sketch and draw from life is frivolous. Remember to protect that time. I started the #walktosee hashtag project on Instagram to build a

community of illustrators who love sketchbooking. Join in by posting your sketchbook drawings and using the hashtag.

7. *You don't have to be a genius.* Notice how much rubbish is out there, then making a picture book might not feel so overwhelming. You don't have to be a genius, just do your thing as well as you can.

8. *Make mistakes.* And recognize when a mistake is a good thing.

9. *Daydream.* Spend time washing up or staring out of windows. Get rid of the dishwasher.

10. *Do the work.* Haruki Murakami likens writing a novel to long-distance running. Making a picture book is similar. Keep going.

11. BLOODY HELL, THINGS WILL GO WRONG. Keep going.

NOT KNOWING
THE RULES
GIVES YOU
GREAT
FREEDOM

Do the work.
Some of it <u>will</u> be rubbish
keep going...

DRAWING FROM LIFE

- Get UNcomfortable.
- Bring the wrong stuff, there is no magical right stuff.
- Get in people's way, it will stop you overthinking.
- Wait until it rains and then start drawing.
- Use body language to tell people if you are up for a chat or not.
- NO FIDDLING. Stop when you are finished.

THINGS I KNOW FOR CERTAIN

- Drawing _feels_ good.

THE END

I like this quote
from Stephen King
in his book 'On Writing.'

'Write ~~with~~ with the door
closed, rewrite with the
door open.'

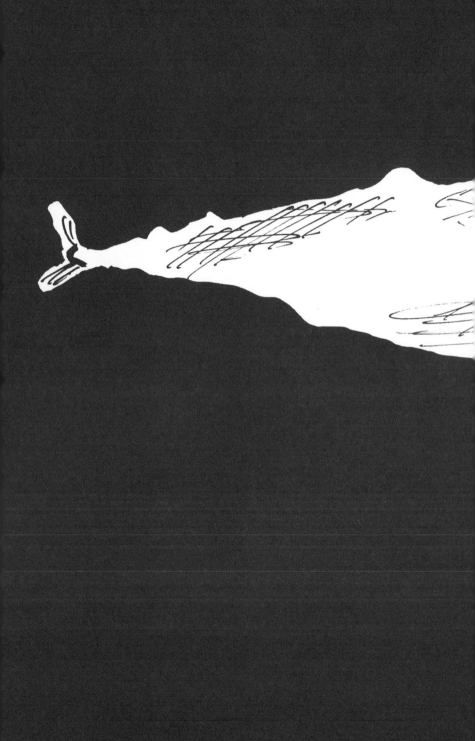

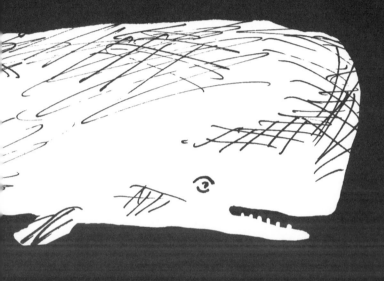

write and draw
  your white whale-
    the one that
    makes your
      heart beat faster.

- Send publishers things they would like to pin on their wall. It is a digital world, but paper is still beautiful.

- Make yourself a nice website/Instagram page.

DRAW ON YOUR
ENVELOPES

BLOODY HELL.

things <u>will</u> go wrong

KEEP

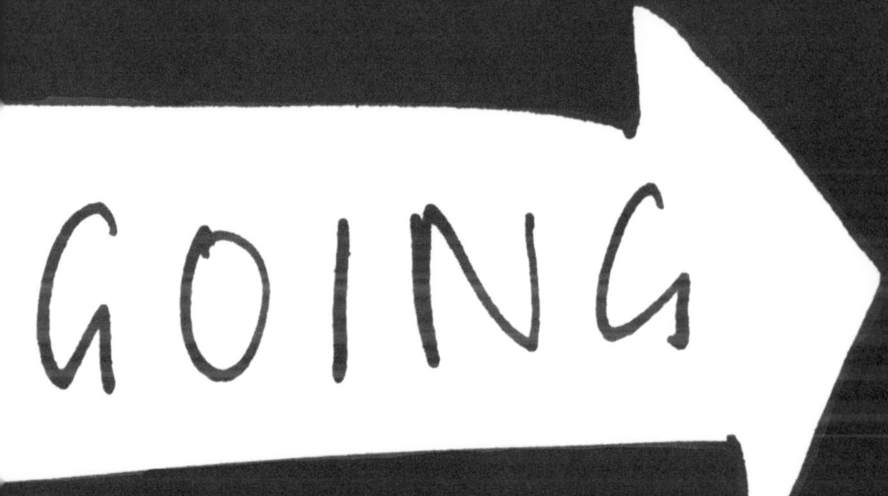
GOING

GOLDEN RULES II

Joanne Harris

These are all things I've learnt during my thirty years as an author. Some I've worked out from experience; some are advice other authors have given me. Either way, I wish I'd known all this when I first started writing. It might have saved me a little time …

1. *Give yourself permission to write.* It isn't an exclusive club. Anyone is allowed to write, for whatever reason. If you love it, do it, and don't allow others to make you feel guilty or ridiculous. And don't fall into the trap of calling yourself an 'aspiring', or 'budding', author or telling people you're not a 'proper' writer. You don't have to be a professional to take what you do seriously. Would you cook a meal for your friends, then apologize that you weren't a 'proper' chef?

2. *Find yourself a writing space.* If you're lucky enough to have an office, or a shed, or a designated writing room, all the better. But a local cafe might work just as well, or a library, or a park bench. Just as long as it suits your purpose, and gets you away from household distractions.

3. *Stop looking for rules.* There aren't any. There's just what works, and what doesn't. And what works for one writer may not work at all for another, even if the books they write are on very similar lines.

4. *Don't chase trends.* Trying to identify what publishers want according to what's currently popular is pointless. Trends come and go very quickly in publishing. By the time you've written your book, the wave will have already passed.

5. *Find yourself a support network.* A writers' group, online or off, or a circle of like-minded friends. Make sure your friends and family know how seriously you take your writing and understand that you need time to pursue it.

6. *Set yourself achievable goals.* Like exercise, writing is best done regularly, and in small doses. Writing for twenty minutes every day is often more realistic than trying to write for hours at the weekend; and if you get into a daily routine, it soon becomes second nature.

7. *Write what you read.* You can't expect to write convincingly in a genre in which you're not a reader.

8. *Work with an editor you trust.* Whether you're a self-published writer or not, whether you're an experienced author or an absolute beginner, you need an editor. Writers who feel they don't need editing are precisely the ones that need it most.

9. *Know your reasons for wanting to write.* Manage your expectations. Most professional authors never make a living from their writing. If your main motivation for writing is the hope of being rich and famous, then you may prefer to choose another hobby.

10. *Be part of the writing community.* Readers, bloggers, editors, publishers, writers and illustrators often interact and work with each other online. They'll welcome you as long as you don't behave in an aggressive, arrogant or entitled manner. And remember – no one owes you anything. To take from the community, you have to give to the community.

Michelle Harrison

On Getting Published.

1. *Prepare for the long haul.* Unless you're *very* talented or lucky, getting published takes time. Most writers rack up a substantial number of rejections before they get anywhere. It took me nearly four to get an agent.

2. *Agents aren't essential.* But in my opinion they're worth every penny of their commission (usually 10–15 per cent). As well as handling tricky things like contracts, agents have good relationships with publishers and are familiar with individual editors' tastes. BUT ...

3. ... even with an agent, you'll still face rejection. A decent agent will stick by you even if your first book – or second or third – doesn't find a publisher. They shouldn't charge any money upfront.

4. *Follow advice, and then don't.* When submitting my first book I read it was best to approach agents who represented similar authors. This got me nowhere. Instead, when I presented my work as something different, that's when they took notice.

5. *Don't rush it.* Spend time on your covering letter and make sure those opening chapters really shine. A great covering letter should include a tantalizing hook for your story, any praise from early relevant readers (family don't count!) and a few details about yourself. Keep it brief and professional. Don't send gifts, gimmicks or illustrations (unless you're a professional artist). Let the writing speak for itself.

6. *Keep your options open.* I spent a year redrafting for one agent who hadn't requested exclusivity, and who ultimately rejected me. It's fine

to query several agents or publishers at once. If asked for the rest of the manuscript, *that's* when you can give an exclusive look.

7. *Ignore those who try to discourage you.*
   'Still writing your little book?'
   'Do you *really* think you're going to get this published?'
   These are comments I heard while writing my first novel. Once your book's out the same people will say they believed in you all along ...

8. *Don't give up.* Rejection stings, but it makes for sweeter success. Go to author talks at festivals and bookshops. Read other writers' publishing journeys. Print out inspiring quotes. Remember, every published writer was once looking for their lucky break, just like you.

9. *Keep your rejections.* You might feel oddly fond of them one day, because each one put you on the path to the right agent or publisher. There's also a practical reason: in the first year I was published I was hit with a large tax bill. My accountant offset this by proving (with my rejections) how long I'd been writing before earning anything.

10. *Believe.* Don't kid yourself that publication will solve all your writing-related insecurities. It'll bring new ones, such as how much marketing spend your book gets, sales (or lack of) and, of course, negative reviews. Hold on to the knowledge that if it happens it's because an entire team at a publisher believed in it as much as you did.

Philip Hoare

1. It must be the first thing you want to do when you wake up. And the last thing you want to do.

2. Write about what you don't know as if you do.

3. Write down that last thing you think of before you go to sleep so you have something to do when you wake up.

4. Walk, run, swim to think.

5. Reading is not a passive but an active, creative act, as Virginia Woolf said.

6. Work a routine if you can. Don't torture yourself.

7. The whole point is to enjoy the process, through the pain. The end point is the end: you can't do anything else after that. So, enjoy the process.

8. Someone said art is imagination acting on experience. I think that's it.

9. Write for yourself and one person you know. Then for everyone else.

10. Ignore all the rules.

A. M. Homes

1. *Don't wait to be ready.* Sometimes you have to write your way into something. Writing is a process of discovery: in order to write something worth keeping, you often have to write through something not worth keeping. Novels aren't like cakes – they don't come out of the oven done.

2. *If you don't make time to write there won't be time to write.* We all lead lives that are much busier and more filled with distraction than they need to be. Make time to write, get up thirty minutes earlier, require yourself to write for twenty minutes a day. Read a physical paper book instead of watching TV. Abandon all social media. Unplug. Don't multi-task. Go for a walk.

3. *Be suspicious of people/students who complete a draft and declare themselves finished.* The first draft is only the beginning. Sober up. There is the writing eye and the editing eye and they are not the same. The writing eye is warm, generous, open-minded, playful, experimental, willing to wander, to adventure. The editing eye asks why this, why here, why now and what exactly are you trying to say and have you done it as well as you could? That said, not every problem can be fixed in one swift motion. I print out my work, read it through and scrawl all over it. I circle things, fix this – wrong order, not clear. There are many passes through a manuscript, many, many revisions.

4. *Feed yourself.* Look at art, listen to music, be in nature. Take in what is happening around you, what are the ideas, conflicts, issues of your time? What is your relationship to them? Do you feel a sense of responsibility to respond, to engage, to take action? Push yourself out of your comfort zone. Ask yourself questions you find hard to answer. Use your writing to explore what you don't understand.

5. *Write what you know.* That's reportedly what writing instructors say, but it makes no sense. No one knows enough to be that interesting over a long period of time. *Write what you don't know.* Write to discover, to understand.

6. *Write what is true for your characters.* You are not your character. Ask what is organic to this character, what he or she was doing before they came to the story (or before you as author showed up). What brought them to this point? Ask what is urgent – why is now the moment you need us (the reader) to pay attention? Why should we drop all else we are doing and come read this story right now?

7. *Write longhand.* It's a better connection hand to brain. Draw. When you get stuck take a piece of plain paper and, without using words, draw the shape of what you are writing in gestural terms. Then ask yourself where you are stuck and how to solve the problem. I often use sketchbooks. I find that writing without lines lets me think in a less linear fashion and more conceptually. I can tell that things are going really well when there I am, writing on different parts of the page; one idea here in the upper left, another over there on the right, fragments, things to remember, sometimes a shopping list, detergent, lemons, more books about ...

8. *Plain paper has no rules.* There are no lines, no borders. Plain paper is about freedom to conceptualize, to wander, to be unbound. The imagination lives to be unbound, to defy our desire for rules, order, control. In order to create we must simultaneously surrender the illusion that we are in control and in the same breath maintain order and structure within the worlds we create. Good Luck!

Nadine Aisha Jassat

1. *Your voice has value.* Your voice is yours and has value, so use it, celebrate it, invest in it, recognize its strengths and growth, listen to it, stay true to it.

2. *Connect to your vision.* Often in creative writing workshops, I ask participants to consider: what do you want your writing to do? What are you going to do for your writing? Your answer doesn't have to be grand – 'I want it to feel freeing' is as good an answer as 'I want to change the world' – it just has to be yours.

3. *It's good to have boundaries, and it's OK to say 'No'.* There can be a pressure to say 'Yes' to everything, but we're all only human, and boundaries can protect you, your time and energy, and your work.

4. *Step away and breathe.* It can be as big as a weekend away wandering in nature, or as small as a cup of tea – but it's important to step away and breathe. These breaks are valuable and can help give you headspace and perspective. Chances are, after a breath of fresh writing air you'll return a lot clearer.

5. *Free yourself in your work.* In the very practice of writing it's important to let it be just you and the page, and allow yourself the freedom to let the story flow. The piece likely has a mind of its own, and its own idea of where it wants to go, so be open, listen to it and let it. Allow yourself to cross genres, to free write, to explore, to be playful and experimental and see where your writing will take you.

6. *Balance your time and energy.* Juggling different areas of life and work and writing can be really hectic, and lots of things that writers do outside of writing – such as readings or workshops – can be amazing but also tiring. So it's important to remember to balance your

writing life, and especially to make time to invest in your creative practice and write.

7. *Invest in creativity more broadly.* Reading, journalling and free writing, visiting an art space, being in nature or doing crafts at home are all good for keeping connected to creativity and fostering a creative energy within you from which your writing can grow.

8. *Listen to your gut.* It's a solid compass, use it!

9. *Look around.* What resources are available to you? Is there a community writing group in your area who could help you energize or give feedback on your work? Or a writing website online with helpful links and tips? Could you join the Society of Authors for advice on contracts and the business side of writing? Does your local library have a quiet workspace to go to when you need a change of scene, or archives/computers/internet access for research and prompts?

10. *Remember it's all a journey.* And you're on yours! So, don't be too hard on yourself, challenge yourself but also have patience and trust in this journey. Remember, too, that how you feel in your writing life could be mirroring or connected to how you feel in other areas of your life, and vice versa, so give yourself time to nurture one, and it might impact the others.

Catherine Johnson

1. What to do? It really only matters to you. No one cares whether you write the thing or not. No one is (rarely, anyway) asking you, begging you, to do it. So you have to do it for you. You're the only person in the whole world this matters to. And you're the only person who'll lose out if you don't do it.

2. Writing saved me. It saved me when the real world was impossible. Keep that little space in your head that's just for you. Not for anyone else, your kids, your partner. Be selfish. It's like having a walled garden you can do and put whatever you like in. Let the grass grow tall. Crouch down and make a den and start pretending.

3. Keep going. Half the battle is not stopping.

4. If you're a joiner-inner find some comrades who'll hold you up.

5. Read everything. Read the really good books that make you gasp and put your head in your hands and think there is no point, but also read the bad books, the ones that make you angry, that make you realize how much better you could do.

6. Remember it's just pretending. Really, really, hard pretending. That's all.

7. Don't worry if you don't have a shed or a hut or a garden room or an office. Don't worry if you only have your kitchen table or your bedroom or your lap. It will be more difficult. But it is possible.

8. The way to learn to write a book is to write a book. Each one's a bit different. If rituals help, fine. Pens, special notebooks, special places to sit, magic knickers. With me it's the opposite. I can't have nice

notebooks. The pressure is too much. The cheaper and shittier the better. Find what works for you.

9.   Never beat yourself up. There are a million people waiting to do it for you. Sometimes, very occasionally, when the good words are falling out of you and it feels more like channelling than anything else, you'll think you are phenomenal. Other times, more often usually, you'll think you are a lost cause, the worst writer that ever lived, the person who can't write one word that isn't terrible. That's normal.

10. A joke:
     Q. Why shouldn't the writer look out of the window in the morning?
     A. Because then they'll have nothing to do in the afternoon.

Trust in yourself, and in the story you want to tell. Keep a routine and do routine things like taking some exercise, cutting down on coffee, getting more sleep. These simple things might not work for you. Some writers would take their espresso intravenously if they could, while others hate even the thought of going for a run. But try to get into good habits, if only for your family and friends. And most advice you might give yourself is both prelude to and part of the main message of the day: *get writing*.

You must do things your own way, but there are some rules that it's good sense to obey. If you want to cross a road without getting knocked down, you really ought to stop, look and listen:

1. *Stop.* Stop over thinking. Stop getting distracted, falling down rabbit holes on the internet, checking the football scores, tidying your desk and arranging your pens. You're procrastinating. No one else will magically write the book for you. It's up to you. Now start.

2. *Look.* Open your eyes. It's not possible to write all the time. Instead of bashing your head against the screen do something productive. Do your research outside today. Stride up a hill, swim in the sea or float in a stream. Sit in a park and let the rain drench your skin. Watch the way the downpour affects other people, running for cover, rushing around with their lives. Are people happily getting soaked? Wonder why. Look about. Ask questions.

3. *Listen.* Be quiet. Listen to your own fears and frustrations, but be brave enough to act against them. Listen to the advice of friends, your agent, your partner, but don't be ruled by it. They will either be right or be wrong, and there's no way of knowing at this stage. But it's your name on the cover of the book when that happy day comes.

It's yours. Make it so. There are many different kinds of writer, and many ways to write a book. Listen to yourself.

I'm more of a reader and curator. I gather treasures and hoard good ideas while risking new ones. Writers around the world have shared some of the things they have learnt, and they have sent me in new directions. So, here's another list of writing advice:

1. *Love your subject.* You ought to enjoy what you're writing about, or at the very least be interested by it. Something on the page has to make you smile. Your writing life will be pretty miserable otherwise. Here's Roald Dahl: 'I began to realize how important it was to be an enthusiast in life. If you are interested in something, no matter what it is, go at it full speed. Embrace it with both arms, hug it, love it and above all become passionate about it. Lukewarm is no good.'

2. *Write every day.* You've got to practise. The more you write, the better you'll get.

3. *Don't get too distracted.* Inspiration is more than just an idea. You have to work hard on that idea and commit time to give it form. You have to concentrate.

4. *Be selective.* Just because you've read a hundred books on a subject, doesn't mean you have to cram all that research in. Leaving out is as important as putting in. Flaubert is said to have once declared 'writing history is like drinking an ocean and pissing a cupful'.

5. *Be patient.* Unless you have the genius of Dickens, success doesn't come overnight. John McPhee says ideas are where you find them. They are everywhere, so trust in yourself to find them, but you also have to work at it. And be patient that your work will find its

readers. Alain de Botton: 'Writing a book is rather like telling a joke and having to wait two years to know whether or not it was funny.'

6. *It's OK to fail.* Have courage. People who don't make mistakes usually don't make anything. Failure at least suggests that you've tried. As Thomas Edison is alleged to have said: 'I have not failed, I've just found 10,000 ways that won't work.' Or, take advice from Samuel Beckett: 'No matter. Try again. Fail again. Fail better.'

7. *Live in hope.* Here's Meg Rosoff: 'Each of us is writing a life story. Every day we write another chapter. Some sections are page turners, cliffhangers, potboilers. Others drone on endlessly without incident – the hero will never fall in love, find a career, figure out how to be a person. Each of us is responsible for imagining the best life possible: the funniest, bravest, most meaningful.'

8. *Do it your own way.* Ray Bradbury: 'I have never listened to anyone who criticized my taste in space-travel, sideshows or gorillas. When such occurs, I pack up my dinosaurs and leave the room.'

And a final thing to add to this, and to all the good advice from others: *don't forget tea and cake.* Writing is tough enough. You don't need to live like a recluse.

Anthony McGowan

Writing books is in many ways like being a deep-sea diver or an astronaut: a lonely, heroic life, cut off from most of humanity, although writers eat more biscuits and are more likely to be on a bender than to suffer from the bends. And just like astronauts and deep-sea divers, survival, for the writer, is all about following a strict set of rules. To deviate from these is perilous; their neglect means falling into the deadly embrace of a giant squid, or floating forever in the cold and dark of deep space. But, luckily, being a writer means you can write your own rules. These are mine:

1. Make an existential leap – tell yourself that you're a writer. Then tell other people. Don't be ashamed of it, be proud. People are genuinely interested. Who would you rather sit next to at a dinner party, the would-be writer or the would-be accountant? No one is going to think you're a fake or a loser because you haven't been published yet.

2. Never begin a book with the sentence, 'A twitch in Roderick's perineum could mean only one thing: it was time to change the awkward-to-reach lightbulb in the oven.'

3. Remember that plot and structure are two different things – think about how you can make a good story better by playing with the chronological sequence, the narrative voice, the point of view and the tense. If this doesn't help, consider ditching the story and trying a new career. We'll always need undertakers and florists.

4. Don't waste time describing things that don't need to be described. Think about what Ezra Pound called the 'luminous details' – small things that help you to see a whole scene, or understand a character. A single 40-watt lightbulb dangling from a bare wire tells you all you need to know about the room. Describe the wart, not the face.

5. Be nice to everyone you meet in publishing. Only geniuses get away with being shits.

6. Avoid the words 'She *felt*' or 'He *thought*': show the characters feeling and thinking. Whenever you see these words, strike them out and start again.

7. Burping in books is never funny; farting is always funny. It's another case of art tracing the lineaments of life. Obviously, timing can transform the merely good into the truly great, just as when at school a fart synchronized to the teacher's low stoop to pick up her fallen chalk is superior to the random fart. However, even the random fart is quite funny. No one ever says to a peacock, 'Hey, Mister, this is neither the time nor the place for that tail ...'

8. If you want to write about food, write when you're hungry. ('Food', here, could be a metaphor ...) This is an instance of art not following life. If you shop when you're hungry you come back with crisps and cake.

9. Read like a maniac. But try not to read only the stuff you find easy and enjoyable. Push yourself. Read classics. Every time you go to the lavatory, read a poem. If it's a short visit, read a short poem. A seventeenth-century Cavalier lyric or a Philip Larkin will do. For longer visits, you have Dante's *Inferno*.

10. The presence of monkeys (or apes) makes even boring books a bit less boring. I've often thought, when stuck in one of the denser passages of *Under the Volcano* by Malcolm Lowry, or during one of those immense paragraphs of Henry James, where nothing much has happened beyond Sir Hubert noticing that the Contessa's

antimacassar has been displaced, that an irruption of apes would greatly improve things.

11. Begin by writing short stories and poems. It's very satisfying to finish a piece of work, and a novel will take you forever. With any luck you'll never have to write one.

12. Think about the reader. Writing is an act of communication. Most writer friends of mine regard their craft as akin to laying an egg. The creative process for them is solitary, and inward-focused. I prefer to think of writing as a conversation. I keep asking my imaginary reader, 'Are you *laughing*? Are you *frightened*? Are you *bored*?'

13. The more you write, the better you get at it. Nearly all first books are terrible.

14. Be careful about doing to excess those things at which you excel. If you're good at description, you'll almost certainly describe too much.

15. Everything in a story should be fully determined, by which I mean that every element must be there for a reason, must serve a function. Does a section of prose illuminate character, move the plot along, help conjure up the world? Does it make the reader laugh or think or gasp in astonishment? Is it beautiful? If not, why is it there? Why are any of us here?

Walking backwards gives a writer a jolt of perspective. It reinforces the reality that, while writing, none of us knows where we are going until we have finished the trip and we look backwards at where we started and where we have managed to get to without knowing where we were headed.

10. *Wear stout shoes.* By which I mean, there are puddles, chasms and the jaws of wild animals into which you are about to walk backwards. Be prepared. Be sensible. (Another way of saying this is: expect the unexpected in any act of writing. If you don't meet something unexpected, you're not actually moving, you're not writing. You're merely taking dictation about something you already know. That's called duplication, not creation.)

9. *Use sunscreen and bring sunglasses.* To be honest, beware the solar glare of mighty muses whose great works inspire you. (I knew someone who wrote fiction at a desk over which loomed a poster-size black-and-white photo of Virginia Woolf. What a mistake. This person could not live up to such a muse and is now in a home for the stunned.)

8. *Ditch the umbrella.* To suggest you might be careful of muse-overload is not to say you should avoid all influences. Encountering a little real-life competition is strengthening. I wouldn't suggest lining those stout boots with bestseller lists from *The Times*, but be aware of who your peers are. Be aware of your peers; it can improve your constitution and your courage. But again: avoid being daunted by your gods and muses.

7. *Read while you walk.* (Not on your electronic device, because you will lose your place and also forget what you've read almost immediately.) Perhaps read something in a different genre from the one in which

you are writing. I read poetry, which I rarely write. I especially read poetry if I am stuck on the path (writer's block: a huge boulder you've backed into because you didn't see it there). Since poetry works by stealth, and makes you leap with surprise, it almost can't help but inch you around a block and get you moving again.

6. *Rest a little.* Put your work aside and have a picnic. But never pack your work in the knapsack out of sight, or you will lose your focus and accidentally end up as a lepidopterist. I always travel with some unfinished piece, and when I unpack it in a hotel room, I leave it out, in case the mocking evidence of my failure-to-date prompts a fresh idea. You want to be ready when that happens. Though there is nothing inherently evil about lepidoptery.

5. *Company.* Is this a recommendation or a prohibition? It's up to you. Some people love chowder-and-marching societies composed of fellows suffering an affliction identical to their own, a support group of writers bumbling backwards together. Others can only forge backwards in doleful solitude. I myself belong to the second category, but I have lots of friends, quite good writers indeed, who meet and discuss and share manuscript pages and plot conundrums. It doesn't seem to hurt them. It's up to you.

4. *Dream.* Daydream, night-dream, doesn't matter. When you pause to rest during your backward itinerary, especially if you are not convinced in which direction you ought next to veer ignorantly, you might ask yourself before sleep a question that vexes you. 'WHY did Melchisidech happen to be carrying a pearl-handled double-action ladies' revolver in that sack of Peruvian corn meal?' 'Why am I writing about the spiritual lives of molluscs?' 'What comes next?' I mean this seriously. Compose a real question. Scribble it on a pad of paper after you unroll your sleeping bag for the night.

Keep it next to you as you doze. You may find that, in the morning, your question has been answered by the serfs and minions of your subconscious, those who work overtime without complaining or charging time-and-a-half, as all decent staff should.

3. *Read your work aloud.* (Though you are still on a backward trek towards an unanticipated destination, I don't recommend reading your work backwards, though I have heard that serious proofreaders read texts backwards to avoid falling into the trap of seeing what they think they should be seeing instead of seeing what is actually there. Tpyos. I mean typos.) Alone in a room, I read my work aloud with a pencil in hand as if I'm at a microphone in a BBC studio. Imagining an audience, I never pause – but at infelicities, confusions, redundancies, boring bits, I make slashmarks in the margin or I circle words that aren't correct. The ear is smarter than the eye, and your ear will hear mistakes that your eye can't see.

2. *Eventually, go back and fix those mistakes.* Preferably before you forget why you had identified eight separate problem lines on the same page.

1. *Notice when you have arrived at your destination.* Don't keep walking backwards into someone else's story. And how will you know your destination when you get there? I can't really say, because I don't know your destination any more than, starting out, you did. But a basic truth of our species, and perhaps a truth of all species, is that home feels like home. A finished story becomes a kind of home. (However, a heads-up: if a photo of Virginia Woolf is hung over the mantelpiece there, you might want to keep going. Just saying.)

1. *Coffee.* Obviously. The psychological benefits of this outweigh the physical. *I have so much work to do*: coffee. *I'm tired*: coffee. *I'm hungry*: coffee with biscuits. *I need to do something for the next ten minutes which isn't staring at the blank screen*: coffee. You get the gist.

2. *A show/series which you can binge-watch.* Honour the need to switch off from the relentless tedium of the world. To watch hours and hours of engrossing crap before settling down to hours and hours of writing literary genius* is an imperative. (*Mediocrity, but let's pretend it will be genius, because otherwise what's the point?)

3. *A bullet journal.* My life has changed since getting one. I am Organized. I carve out time, between the dotted lines, for work, friends and family (in that order, unfortunately). Planning my days, weeks and months means not having to face the crippling anxiety of the question: *how will I ever do everything*? It is all do-able, if managed well.* Keep the relationships you have strong by making time for the people who matter. (*She says from under her desk, pretending deadlines aren't happening.)

4. *Be quiet, be alone.* Have you done nothing for an hour? Maybe two? A whole day? Maybe even a week or five? That's OK. Ideas don't often come when you're busy planning, scurrying about or socializing. They usually come in the quiet of the night, in moments of solitude and contemplation. Be alone. Solitude is an excellent recipe for creativity. Listen to radio shows that spark thought and imagination – it comes second only to reading.

5. *Temper your solitude with people.* But find the right ones. The ones who will tell you you're brilliant (even when you're average), and who then perhaps give instruction on how you can become more brilliant

(above average). Be with the ones who will listen and understand the trials of being a writer, but also who have no idea what it's like, because it's good to escape from it once in a while (see tip number 2).

6. *Plan the story.* It doesn't work for everyone, but having written my own novels and been a ghost-writer, I've learnt the merit of structure and how that can focus your writing. Just a few lines for each chapter and a character profile will see you through those blank days. The plot might change, but that's OK too. Pencilling it out can also help to show the flaws in the story before you've even begun. Would you ever go on holiday without booking the tickets or a place to stay? Then why embark on what might be a year-long journey without knowing where you're going? Unless you're a particularly adventurous person, in which case I'm thoroughly envious.

7. *Set a target.* To avoid the anxiety of having to write a 100K novel in two weeks, give yourself a weekly writing target (mine is usually 1,500 words, every day, Monday–Friday). If you don't have a contractual deadline, give yourself a (sensible) target anyway. Know your limits. If you can't write 1,500 words a day, that's fine, as long as you write what you can (bearing in mind that stretch of time when you might not want to do anything).

8. *You've heard it before: read well.* Read lots. Read outside your comfort zone. Drink in words that inspire, swallow a story's structure, breathe in a well-crafted character, absorb the heady mix of creative storytelling and beautiful writing.

9. *Character, character, character.* Think of all the books you remember loving, is it the story you recall or the characters who brought that

story to life? Slip into your characters' shoes, have conversations between them in your head (or out loud, whichever feels more dramatic). You don't have to name their hopes and fears, or the first pet they had, but make sure you know them. Reading is intimacy. Be intimate with your characters.

10. *Get it done.* Finish the first draft without looking back and editing. Over-editing can be the death of a book. Writing all the way through, getting to the finish line, gives you a solid foundation. You may (probably will) hate it, but then slowly, steadily, you'll build upon that foundation and learn to like it, until you finish carving in the details and find, finally (hopefully), that you love it.

Kiran Millwood Hargrave

If you'd asked me seven years ago, when I first started taking my practice seriously, what I considered myself to be, I would have told you I was a writer. For a while after my first book was published, I called myself an author. Now, and ever after, I think of myself as a storyteller. Some of you may be thinking, why does it matter what I call myself? But we're in the business of stories, and words matter. Here are ten tips for *storytellers*, or rather, what works for me:

1. Read widely, often, attentively, and for pleasure.

2. Write first drafts fast, like fire is licking your wrists.

3. Edit slow, like drifting on a raft in an endless sea.

4. Get a cat.

5. Or a dog – use the walks to think.

6. Stretch every half hour.

7. Find people who take your work seriously, and talk about it with them.

8. Back up your hard drive.

9. Protect your writing time rabidly.

10. Read your work aloud – this is how you find the heat.

Whether I'm writing for children, teenagers or adults, the central tenet of telling my reader a story prevails. I revel in language, but not at the cost of not carrying readers along, and making them care. This to me is what a great novel is: a great story.

For me, the title of storyteller allows for growth and playfulness in a way writer or author doesn't. When I was a writer, I existed in a land of maybes. When I was an author, I existed in a land of books, where my words were encased between covers. As a storyteller, my tales are never more alive than when they are in the act of being read, preferably out loud.

Which leads me to the last of my tips, and the most vital one I have for any would-be teller of tales: *read aloud*. The work of others and your own words. Without breath, stories cannot truly live. And who of us does not want our worlds to come alive for our readers, for all the possible years to come?

David Mitchell

1. It's OK to be unsure what a story is about until you've finished the first MS. Don't let the question 'Yes, but what are my themes and ideas?' be a roadblock. These can be foregrounded in the rewrite. You can't improve a blank page. Get the story down, however scrappy and full of holes it is.

2. It's a process, not a disaster, to realize, fifty or a hundred pages in, that you've taken a wrong turn and need to begin again. Your glorious edifice may turn out to be the scaffolding, after all. Good. You'll need scaffolding.

3. Plot and character provide momentum for the journey. Ideas, good lines and flashes of beauty make the journey worth going on.

4. In fiction, parentheses are a tax on the reader's attention. This tax costs more to collect than it earns in revenue. If your thinking is uncluttered, you'll never need them.

5. Exclamation marks in prose are like people who laugh at their own jokes! The fewer the better! Except, of course, when writing characters who laugh at their own jokes!

6. Beware too many sentences beginning with the word 'I'. They get as tiring on the page as they are in a bar.

7. 'Seem' is a word that sits on the fence. 'Although and 'Though' are unpersuasive ways to start a sentence.

8. Self-esteem and self-belief are well and good, but if you start believing your own publicity, you're doomed. Fake humility is boastier than boastfulness.

9. Advice for people swallowed jointly by a whale on a collaborative project: don't interrupt, and begin responses with 'And' rather than 'But'. An interruption says, 'Listening to you isn't worth my precious time.' The word 'But' is a tiny, admonitory slap. Poor ideas will wither on the vine by themselves; or, the poor idea may bloom into a far richer idea than you initially suspected. This advice can be fruitfully applied to relationships, too. Classic Two-fer.

10. Submit every metaphor and simile in your work to the now-universal 1- to 5-star review. The 5- and 4-star imagery can stay: everything else is out. If you can't decide whether it's a 3-star or a 4-star, it's a 3-star, and should be chucked.

11. Don't let a quest for perfection keep you inside the whale's belly forever. Out with it. Come on.

12. If you're stuck, it's often because you don't know the character/s well enough. The story isn't going anywhere anyway, so spend a little time with the people in it.

13. Epic midnight writing sessions are a young writer's game. Losing the next day to naps and grogginess is a net loss.

14. Break any rule about writing in this book if you've understood why its author found the rule helpful, and if your narrative requires you to break it. This is how arts and sciences evolve.

Congratulations: you are a writer. By reading this, the decision has already been made. And even if you don't think you're a writer you are one – you just haven't embarked on the act of exorcism that is the transference of thoughts and ideas on to the page. Beyond that, however, it's a guessing game for all concerned. There is no correct way to write, no more than there is a correct way to think or to throw a burning cat into a duck pond from a tenth-floor window.

All that can be offered are a few pointers from those who have been in the abyss, survived the abyss and keep returning to the abyss, which brings me neatly to my first point: it's OK to repeat words. Because writing is casting spells, and spells rely on repetition, rhythm. When it works, it's a form of magic. And also ignore your teachers: it is fine to start a sentence with the word 'because'. And also 'and'. Twice in one paragraph, even. Rules are for breaking.

Here then are some other thoughts I have jotted down during twenty years in the ... not the abyss. Four times is just excessive. Let's call it the *void*.

1. Start small. The Venus de Milo was once an unremarkable lump of stone.

2. Blood may be shed, but the human body is remarkable at regeneration.

3. Quicken your reader's heartbeat.

4. Eat your greens.

5. Steal and be stolen.

6. Novels rarely begin at the beginning. A spider weaves its web from the centre.

7. Do some physical labour. Move rocks, chop wood, bake a cake.

8. Sometimes you must offend people.

9. Sometimes you must offend yourself.

10. Get underneath the story and look at the engine from below.

11. Watch Werner Herzog's *Fitzcarraldo*. Your book is the boat. You are Klaus Kinski. You're covered in mud and everyone hates you. Now push.

12. Less is best. Edit.

13. Move into a different room and drink a large glass of water.

14. If you are stuck in a dead-end street go back thirty pages and write yourself a doorway.

15. Coffee: don't drink the cheap stuff.

16. Remember: you are part of a noble tradition.

17. Stroke a dog.

18. D. H. Lawrence was dismissed for most of his career and his obituaries were overwhelmingly hostile. He wrote exactly what he wanted. He remains in print today.

19. Change the font.

20. Success and money are unrelated.

21. Fashion is fleeting but good writing is forever.

22. Chaos is rarely conducive. Find a neutral space.

23. 'Anger is an energy' – John Lydon.

24. Everyone has a book inside them. Most should remain there.

25. No one ever left a library a lesser person.

26. Walking is writing with your feet. Walk often.

27. Make up a new word. They all come from someone, somewhere.

28. Let doubt be your umbrella in the rainstorm.

29. You've probably repeated yourself repeated yourself.

30. Sleep well if you can.

31. Buy some bird feeders. Fill them. Watch the birds.

32. A novel is never finished. The art is in knowing when to stop.

33. Now go back and replace every word with a different one.

34. Try to be a better person.

35. Never, ever, ever, ever, ever give up.

REFLECTING

THE WIDE WORLD
Jan Morris

Last week I celebrated my ninety-third birthday. Despite creeping senility, of course I'm still writing and today it's about maps.
I've spent much of my writing life thinking about the spirit of
place, and as a result my house in Wales is infested with maps.
It is not a large house, and they are inescapable.

For a start there is an entire book stack of books about
cities, each with its map, and another overflowing with world
guidebooks; they include a whole shelf of Baedekers, from 1888
to the present day, and the old ones in particular are equipped
with delectable cartography. Then there are twelve battered
box-files of city maps from around the world, Alexandria to
Zagreb by way of Marrakesh, and a dozen more of miscellaneous
topography, and a big American globe on its revolving stand,
and a very large map of Wales on a wall.

Four drawers overflow with British Ordnance Survey maps,
supplemented by a bound volume of the entire four-inch series,
and there are nine successive editions, all in a row, of *The Times
Atlas of the World*. The first dates from 1922 and they include
the five-volume midcentury edition of 1958, for which I myself
contributed the title. There are nine or ten international atlases,
too, varied of date, nature, purpose, language and range – one
is an *Atlas of the Moon*, and much the most spectacular is the
mighty *Atlas of Wales*.

Oh, they are all sorts and conditions, my maps, and they
have their own stories. Look, here is Lloyd George's own copy
of the *Historical Atlas of Palestine*, dated 1915. As Prime Minister
he advised General Allenby to use it during his campaign to

capture Jerusalem in the very next year. Have you noticed that handkerchief map of New York City behind the door there? You can crumple it up in your handbag as you wander around Manhattan, or even blow your nose in it. And do you feel that bump beneath the carpet underneath your feet? That's the elegant *Atlas of Egypt,* printed in Giza by order of His Majesty King Fouad I in 1928. I store it there to keep it properly flat, and under other rugs around the house sleeping maps are preserved with the same intent.

Infestation? Well, but benediction too: my maps bring in to our house the permanent blessings of friends, memories and places, sent to us here in kindness, I like to think, from time and the wide world.

Reading books of travel by other writers is another source of inspiration. My two favourite are Alexander William Kinglake's *Eothen,* published in 1844, and Charles Doughty's *Travels in Arabia Deserta,* from 1888. And the two books' attitude to maps say a lot about their authors. Kinglake, although he took immense care in the writing of his book, and although the complicated journey he describes took him through a wide swathe of the Arab East, wrote as he travelled, in a spirit of gentlemanly merriment, and he addressed it simply to *One of his Friends.* It is the greatest fun, and 'the only hard word in it', he says, is its title. It contains no map at all.

Doughty's book is seldom read by anyone all the way through, being immensely long and written in a complex neo-antique kind of English prose, peculiar to itself. It describes in profound, scholarly detail his travels, often perilous, through the Arabian desert, dressed and living as an Arab himself, and reflecting the society and the styles of its peoples as they had never been described to the West before. It contains a single truly beautiful map of Northwestern Arabia, in three colours, and in the book's very latest edition this is published in a separate binding. It is attributed to Charles Doughty himself, thirty-two miles to the inch, presented to the RGS, and it perfectly reflects both his own character, and the nature of his great book.

I dearly love both books – in all I have nine copies of them in different editions. It is telling, though, *pace* dear laughing Kinglake, that it is the opening lines of *Arabia Deserta* that I often find myself, to music of my own invention, singing in my bath.

BENEATH THE SURFACE
Carsten Jensen

To me, inspiration is a child of discipline. I don't hang around waiting for lightning to strike. I sit down every morning in front of the screen.

And it's always the screen, except for when I'm taking notes. For these I use beautiful little handmade notebooks: I have a huge collection which I bought in Jaipur five years ago and still hasn't run out. It's my little tribute to the romantic idea of the writer. I write in them when inspiration suddenly strikes. But then, it's back to the screen.

In the last stage of a novel I'll discard huge chunks. Every time I do that I'll think, there goes a whole year of work. If I'd known that would happen while I was writing I couldn't have gone on. You must always write under the illusion that what you write is brilliant. And you must always drop that illusion when you edit.

Don't compete. Don't say to yourself, I want to be the best. Say to yourself: I want to do the best I can. That's all. Do your best. It sounds so banal. But I can think of no better advice. I did my best. As a writer you need delusions of grandeur, and you need realism. The challenge is finding the balance between them.

Be humble – even though deep down you are an arrogant bastard. You must be, because how else would you dare impose your words and visions on others? Who asked for them? Nobody. But still, there you are, writing words that you want to be read.

I can write anywhere if the situation demands it. A few weeks after the fall of the Taliban, back in early 2002, in Kandahar, I sat with my laptop on the floor of an automechanic's workshop. It was the only place I could find a generator. When I was reporting from Afghanistan I discovered the therapeutic function of writing. Whenever I focused on a story I was able to keep my fear at bay. Writing was like going through a dark tunnel focusing on the light ahead. Sitting in front of my laptop, I imposed order on chaos and carved meaning out of meaninglessness. And that's what all writing is about.

I think all writers should choose an animal to emulate. Mine is the East African naked mole-rat, which is ugly as hell, appears immune to the ageing process and lives deep underground, where it can survive without oxygen longer than any other mammal. That's my aim as a writer: to dig deep beneath the surface of the mind and survive in places where most people can't breathe.

I once wrote an epic novel about sailors and the sea called *We, the Drowned*. Often readers who love sailing approach me hoping we'll have a nice chat about all that we have in common. But I don't love sailing: it actually bores me. Experience and fiction aren't the same thing, I tell them – and so they go away disappointed. My conclusion: never meet the writer.

Can I live without reading? Definitely not. Can I live without writing? I don't know. I've never tried. As a child I was swallowed by a writer.

A RED SUITCASE
Onjali Q. Rauf

In my bedroom, buried deep inside a large wooden chest stuffed with Memories-I-Can't-Throw-Away (posters of Frodo, Gandalf and Keanu Reeves are for life, surely?), is a small, red suitcase.

This suitcase, despite my every intention to traverse with it through Europe in a glamorous 1920s version of travel that only exists in my head, has never once seen the light of day. For all its swanky leather straps and hot-diggity wheels, it has been stashed in the deepest, darkest regions of my room for nigh on twenty years, where no one but my writing gremlins and I can reach it: because inside, stuffed to breaking point, lie a thousand paper carcasses.

Let me explain. Becoming a writer requires bodies – bodies of ideas, words, scribblings, even entire books That Didn't Make It. Hundreds if not thousands of sheets that mark hours, days, weeks, months and even years spent writing stories that Just Weren't Good Enough for human consumption.

Every writer I have been so fortunate to meet has some form of this Case of Literary Carcasses – it might be hidden under their bed or in a drawer; it might have its own attic room or even its own World War II bunker buried deep in the back garden, or be sneakily stashed away in a hyper-drive. But believe me, they exist in every writer's home. And chances are, each will only grow in size – no matter how many books their owner may have published already, or if they're still striving to reach the Promised Land of Print.

For years, my Case of Literary Carcasses haunted me: a box-shaped testament to my failures. I suppose it didn't help that along with the bodies of started-but-eternally-stopped stories, I had to add countless rejection letters from agents who all agreed with my red suitcase. Rejections that served as a reminder to me and my writing gremlins that we Simply Weren't Good Enough Yet. That maybe, just maybe, we were writing up the wrong tree.

But my red suitcase also pushed me on – and I know for a fact your own stash of hidden notes and unwanted rejections will push you on too. If one idea, or chapter, or character, or story isn't working, you go on until you find the ones that do. You will cry, you will want to give up, you will scare your family and friends with your ravings about what it's all for, but the writing gremlin inside you won't allow you to give up. So you *let* the carcasses pile up, you *let* the rejection letters stream in, until you Do It: you find the story the world tells you it's ready for.

My bright red suitcase is soon going to be added to by a bright blue one (poor thing thinks it's off for a holiday soon, and has no idea of what's coming). I suppose I could throw the pages of my failures into a recycling bin – along with those rejection letters – but I don't want to. The pain is a reminder of the journey that needed to be taken.

It's taken me nearly two decades, but I've finally also come to realize that my red suitcase and its equivalents aren't freaky or abnormal. They're a sign you belong to a fellowship that is built on countless failures, but which never stops trying to create something worthwhile to bring to the world. So go on creating those paper carcasses, and let your red suitcase – no matter its disguise – push you on. You never know where they, and your pesky inner writing gremlins, might take you ...

CREATIVE PATHS
Dan Kieran

My experience of the writing – or perhaps simply a *creative* – life is that it is a warrior's path and a worrier's path. You have to be brave and you have to accept the worry. It was ever thus I'm afraid. If you want to be rich, go and work in the city. Or become a lawyer. But if you do, by the time you realize you are alive you will realize the gold is behind you.

I usually hesitate to advocate the life-path I chose, which was actually not a path until I decided to walk in that direction, because there have been times in my life that have been incredibly dark and difficult. But that reluctance assumes it would have been lighter and easier if I'd always been able to rely on a regular wage, which I do not believe. Besides, if you are reading this book then you probably are on the creative path yourself, or you want to be and just need a push. Well consider this as one. You won't regret it. But you do have to let the path take you where it wants you to go.

It was not wanting to walk a path others had trodden before that saved me. I'm convinced of that. I dropped out of university. Twice. The first time to contend with a mental health issue I have since come to terms with (rather than recovered from). I'm forty-three now and I believe that if you haven't had some kind of mental health crisis by the time you are forty you are not paying attention. Life is insane. Make sure you give yourself the time and space to have one.

The second time I dropped out of university towards the end of the 1990s was to work for free at a magazine called *The Idler*. Everyone around me thought I was mad, but it was obviously the correct decision from a creative point of view. If you follow the creative compass in your heart you will always find a way. Even if the way does not lead to fame and fortune, as you hope, but requires you to change your perspective on what matters in the deep well of your soul instead, which it will. I guarantee you that. In my experience success doesn't really teach you anything. Only failure does that.

I have no qualifications and no degree so I have never had any kind of safety net to fall back on. But this lack of a safety net turned out to be my safety net. Because when you have nothing to rely on you have nothing to lose so you are prepared to take on seemingly ridiculous obstacles. That's how my creative life has led me on a journey that took in the experience of learning to code (despite failing miserably in maths at school) and launching the first *Idler* website that evolved into co-writing a bestselling book called *Crap Towns*, to then spending a year trying to get arrested for a book about Tony Blair's policy of criminalizing peaceful protest under the guise of defeating terrorism for a book called *I Fought the Law*, and then driving across England in a milk float for a book and BBC Radio 4 programme called *Three Men in a Float*.

And on to today and the desk I find myself writing this on in the office of Unbound, a book-publishing platform I founded with two friends nearly a decade ago, which has forty-five employees today. Again, this was something I did because I had nothing to lose after the global financial crisis of 2008. And don't go thinking starting and running a company is not a creative act. It's actually been the most challenging and fulfilling creative project I've ever embarked on. I don't say this lightly, or out of bravado, but the books we've published have demonstrably changed the world.

So that all sounds marvellous, right? That's the warrior bit. That's the version of me who does talks on stages and coerces words to represent me in the best way I know how on the page. But you have to learn to handle and accept the worrier's path that inevitably runs alongside a life of adventure, because you are choosing that one too. While all that other stuff sounds wonderful and exciting, which it was and is, I estimate there have probably only been about four or five years in the last twenty when I've been completely relaxed about paying the rent and making sure my three beloved children have what they need. We've also only had a handful of fancy holidays. Only once so far have I actually hit the buffers and had to beg and borrow enough money to keep everything together. I've also been forced to take a few minimum wage jobs here and there, which was humiliating at the time but vitally educational in retrospect. Everything has always turned out OK though. The worst times seemingly propelling me into the most rewarding ones of all.

I'd be lying if I didn't admit I'd had a fuck-ton of anxiety, therapy and sleepless nights over the years, though. But less, less and fewer, I'd wager, than if I'd spent the last twenty years in a job I didn't like, while living a life that wasn't my own. Not that I'll ever know.

One last thing, which is why living creatively is more important than your creative output itself, is that living a creative or fulfilling life also makes you more likely to find love. Imagine yourself as a tuning fork. If you live a creative life you are vibrating at the same frequency as the Universe itself. That's what I think. And if you are playing your authentic tune, you will attract others playing theirs too.

A LONG GAME
Wyl Menmuir

If you've chosen to write a novel, you're playing a long game. It may take a year, two years, five years, ten, to see it through to completion. It takes discipline and resolve to shape and polish your idea until it gains something of that luminous quality you imagined it emitting when you first conceived of it. For much of the time, far from luminous, it will feel shapeless and unpolishable, and this is when the dinner invitation, the new TV series, your Twitter feed, the idea for the next novel that is definitely going to be better than the one you're working on now, all begin to look increasingly tempting.

When writing a first draft, give yourself a daily word count and when you're editing, an amount of time you'll spend on the novel each day. Treat both as sacrosanct, even – or rather especially – if you only have time to fit in ten or fifteen minutes after the day job, after the children have fallen asleep, after your partner has sloped off to bed.

Temper discipline with kindness. After each hard-won 10,000 words you complete, and certainly after each completed draft, take a walk in the woods, surf, spend a couple of hours in an isolation tank, whatever floats your boat. Build in small celebrations to remind you that you're making progress. And be kind to those around you. If you want to complain about how terribly gruelling writing is, find another writer and moan it out together, though perhaps even limit this to ten minutes per conversation. Your partner/friends/children don't need to hear it.

Take your novel for regular walks. Talk through the storyline to yourself aloud (it has to be aloud for some reason, so if you worry about what others think, ensure your walk is somewhere remote). Talk to yourself about the problems you're encountering with plot, the characters and their lives, their motivations and frustrations, the novel's emerging themes, and when you come back to your desk, you'll find you have something to write where it may have seemed there was nothing before.

Some days you may be entirely absorbed by your project, lost to it in a state of transcendent flow, but be prepared for the grind, for the hours of sanding down through the grades with little reward or sign of progress. Be prepared, too, that at some point you may also lose belief in the piece entirely. As novelist Liz Jensen told me when I despaired of a novel I was working on, 'You may have lost all hope, but you can still keep your appointment with the manuscript.' Flow and despair and everything in between are transient states; all that matters is that you push on.

I have one piece of advice that I find so helpful I had it carved into the surface of my writing desk: *Finish what you start.* It's a daily reminder that I need to keep going until I find the right words to express what is essentially ineffable, and that however formless the piece is right now, I will eventually discover the shape it needs to assume.

SOME SYMBOLS
Sita Brahmachari

The potency of writing comes to me most often in dreams. Each time I set out to write a book I doubt that it's possible to contain this unconscious into something that might one day have form enough to become a poem, play, short story or novel.

Stories first emerge to me through symbol, and these symbols often have the human heart, spirit and nature at their core (the artichoke charm, the dawn owl, the skep-heart, jasmine flowers, rivers). These symbols attach themselves to characters who walk through the portal of my imagination. Often I don't know how or why the symbols are clinging on to them and it's part of my own treasure hunt of the imagination to discover why each one belongs to a character. Perhaps even they don't know why, and the discovery might be the journey of the story.

Symbolic worlds and the landscapes of belonging of my characters are closely connected. First, I take them to the places that they feel most at home in and then to the locations where they presently find themselves in the journey of my story. I am forensic in wanting to get inside the minds, hearts, dreams, food preferences, smells and musical tastes of my characters, and I prefer to get to know them as if I am meeting a stranger. I think it's my patience in getting to know them that later leads me to be offered the richness of their stories. In early drafts, I may not be conscious of the golden threads that will be the connective tissue of my story, but later when I look back I see that this is the groundwork of writing for me: fully immersing myself in symbol and character leads me to discover the golden threads.

I like to write characters' voices in dialogue with each other; to test what happens when different combinations of characters meet. I ask what would bring these people together. I'll find a tension or conflict point, small or large, and test them grappling in conversation together. Quite often these early scenes will end up leading me to the core scenes in the plot that I could not have come to by planning. This is where I know if I have inhabited a voice, caught a character's rhythm of speech, their symbolic world, references and word preferences. When I can dream my characters' dreams the nuanced plot-jewels begin more fully to unfold to me.

Becoming awake to the story comes through the neck-aching, eye-straining, time-warping graft of writing and editing at the desk. I will agonize over the rhythm of a line and am never finished in attempting to distil the word hoard to kindle enough for a reader to want to enter, but not too much. It's a messy process of ups and downs; excitement, illumination and dejection, all shared with patient, and frankly brave, editors! But if the symbolic world is alive, I know that the story's beating heart will eventually lead me home.

READ SOME MORE
Sarah Moss

'Being a writer' is not a sound ambition. Writers are not a distinct species. Writing is work, not a lifestyle choice. Some of us write on trains, at the kitchen table late at night, in meetings when we're pretending to take notes, during lunchbreaks from shops, hospital wards and building sites, while the baby or the elderly parent is having a nap. We might be wearing uniforms, suits, pyjamas, frilly floral dresses from Marks & Spencer. All that we have in common is a commitment to the practice of literature.

If you want to be rich and famous, marry into an oligarchy or display yourself on YouTube or something. Go into high finance, turn a democracy into a dictatorship (but don't do that). If you want to write, *read*.

Read some more. Read books you find uncomfortable and difficult. It doesn't matter what you like, read what's good, and if it doesn't please you, work out exactly why. (It's fine to dislike Henry James, I dislike Henry James, but I understand why he's a good writer and what the rest of us can learn from him.) 'I don't like it' is not literary criticism and you won't learn from it.

Read some more. Read about unfamiliar times and places, about people who are not like you. Read in all the languages you can, and read in translation. You're looking for windows, not mirrors, and for ways of using words you haven't seen before.

As you write, try things that probably won't work. You're probably right that they won't work, but you might not be, and if you're wrong you've found something new. Experiment. Play. Make mistakes. Be ambitious. It will all go wrong but you'll learn how to write better.

Delete your work and try again. Fail better. Your time is precious to you but completely irrelevant to the quality of the finished work. If your characters start to feel autonomous, it doesn't mean you've become the handmaiden of the muse, it means you're writing stereotypes. By all means write with your guts, but keep your intellect on. The reader doesn't want to see your guts.

Your feelings don't matter. You can write excellent work about which you feel terrible and terrible work about which you feel excellent. Sometimes you'll think your writing has just redefined the capacities of language and sometimes you'll think you've brought shame on everyone you've ever met. Both of these thoughts are the ego's white noise. Just show up to work and do the job.

Plumbers don't get plumber's block, doctors don't get doctor's block, waiters don't get waiter's block. Just write the damn thing. You can delete it later.

A FEW WORDS
Raynor Winn

How can I tell anyone how to write? I'm not a writer. I just got up one day and thought I'd put a few words on a page to make a record of an event, then got completely carried away. But what I can do, unquestionably well, is tell you how not to write, the things to absolutely avoid, and the best ways to get it entirely wrong.

There was a famous female author – see, I'm not even very good at referencing – who said that if you're going to write, that is really write, you need your own room to do it in. Well, that's great if you live in a manor house in the country. But most of my writing has been done in a two-room apartment. So, I've written at the kitchen table, while peeling potatoes, training the puppy to fetch the ball and keeping out of the way of my husband who was in the other room trying to finish the project for his degree, and couldn't work unless he was listening to Radio 3. I'm not a fan of Radio 3. The only place to guarantee some silence and total space to work is in my own head. I've found this strange way of completely blanking out everything that's happening around me and focusing entirely on the words, to enter the world the words are portraying. A room of my own. But possibly not quite what the author had in mind when she was looking out over her beautiful garden.

If you've never had anything to do with publishing, or don't know anyone who has, or come from another era, or like me put down the screwdriver one day after rewiring a light switch and thought – 'I know, I'll write a book' – then you won't know about publicity. You'll go through the agonizingly long process of getting the words on the page, then the nerve-racking roller-coaster ride of getting those words into print and think that's it, you've made it, you're an author now and all you have to do is sit back and watch your work of art fly off the shelves. You're so wrong. Now you have to sit in front of hundreds of people and explain yourself. Wring out a meaning from the words in a way that hopefully all those faces looking back at you can understand. That's when it will hit you. Why, oh why did I write that scene? If I hadn't written a sex scene set on a beach, I wouldn't have found myself sitting on a chair on a raised stage under a spotlight, trying to answer a question about mid-life sex. So, if you don't want to find yourself in that position, then be really careful which words you choose to put on the page.

The day will come when you've successfully climbed the mountain with your book, it's sold a few copies, you've achieved your life's ambition and you think that from here on life will be a gentle sail into the sunset, with a nice glass of something to help you on the way. Right at that point, when you're off guard, the publisher will ask you how the next book is coming along. You'll be really flattered and sign on the line, party for a week, then forget about a looming deadline because you're too busy with the publicity for the previous book. Until that is, possibly just six months before the day when the manuscript should be handed over to your editor as your polished pride and joy, you type in the title 'Book 2' on page one. Of course, if you're a real writer, this won't happen, you'll take the whole experience in your stride with a well-balanced timetable, no last-minute panics and instead perfect, flawless prose.

There are so many places to find advice on the writing life, so many versions of the route to publishing utopia. Only you can draw your map, by taking all the wrong turns and every misdirection you find along the way. All you can do is let the words guide you and if they're the right words in the right order they'll take you to your destination. And if they don't, you can always finish the rewiring and be glad you didn't share the details of your sex life with a hundred thousand strangers.

ROLL THE DICE
Tom Gauld

THE RECLUSIVE AUTHOR TELLS US ABOUT HIS WRITING DAY

I WAKE AT THE SAME TIME EVERY DAY AND, AFTER A BREAKFAST THAT I AM UNWILLING TO DISCUSS, GO TO A ROOM THAT I WILL NOT DESCRIBE AND WRITE IN A MANNER THAT I DO NOT WISH TO TALK ABOUT.

PEOPLE OFTEN ASK ME IF I USE A TYPEWRITER, A WORD PROCESSOR OR A PEN. I NEVER TELL THEM.

WHEN I HAVE WRITTEN A SPECIFIC NUMBER OF WORDS, I STOP. THE WAY I CHOOSE TO SPEND THE REST OF THE DAY IS A PRIVATE MATTER.

THE RECLUSIVE AUTHOR WILL NEITHER CONFIRM NOR DENY THAT AN AS-YET-UNTITLED NEW BOOK MAY, OR MAY NOT, BE PUBLISHED AT SOME POINT IN THE NEAR, OR FAR, FUTURE.

1851: HERMAN MELVILLE CONSIDERS A TITLE FOR HIS NEW NOVEL

THE WHALE?

MOBY-DICK?

OF WHALES AND MEN?

EVERYTHING YOU ALWAYS WANTED TO KNOW ABOUT WHALING BUT WERE AFRAID TO ASK?

AHAB AND MOBY'S EXCELLENT ADVENTURE?

MEN ARE FROM MARS WHALES ARE FROM VENUS?

WHERE'S MOBY?

GOLDEN RULES III

1. 'Take your time.' This has to be the most important advice, and it was passed on to me by Nobel Laureate Nadine Gordimer. She had been speaking in Oxford, about writing and truth. Afterwards, as she signed books, she asked what I was working on. I'd met her previously in very different circumstances, during my first visit back to Johannesburg after twenty-six years in exile. That earlier time, I found her dealing with sleeping arrangements and timetabling before we clambered on to a bus for a weekend conference of the Congress of South African Writers at a centre out in the bush. It was 1991, a year after Nelson Mandela's release, and I was reconnecting with the land of my birth, having already set two novels there. *Journey to Jo'burg* had only recently been 'unbanned'. Her advice has constantly reassured me that writing is part of a wider life.

2. Notebooks are essential companions for thoughts, images, details, questions. I use two or three for the long-distance journey of a novel. Once I've jotted something down, I know it's there and my mind is free to roam.

3. Listen with your inner ear during research and when writing. It takes time to filter out the noise and hear the essence.

4. Observe with your inner eye. It can take time to filter out clutter.

5. Daydream your story and characters. Daydreaming can't be rushed!

6. If you create lots of drafts, don't worry. Don't compare your process to that of a writer with the speed of a hare. Your course is your own to shape and reshape, to thread, weave, loosen or tighten, finding its integrity.

7. Seek out trusted readers. As many of my characters have life experiences that are different from my own, I frequently return to key people from my research journey to share a near-final draft. May you also have good fortune with editors whose critical encouragement spurs you on, especially in the final lap.

8. If you find the 'wrong' title stuck in your head, don't be afraid to seek help. I wrote *The Other Side of Truth* under the working title 'Dare to Tell'. Those three words kept repeating themselves like an old gramophone needle trapped in a scratch on the disc. I knew that I wanted 'Truth' in the title and put out the call to a few trusted readers. When a friend offered a list of suggestions, *The Other Side of Truth* leapt out at me. Her family had been part of my initial inspiration, so the knot was tied. I love reading other writers' acknowledgments, not only for potential insights into the creation of a particular work but also for the reminder that all writers need networks of support.

9. Read widely. Don't limit yourself. In our market-oriented world, it's easy to be caught in a 'brand'. Explore different forms, genres ... and experiment.

10. Trust yourself to stay the course. My favourite proverb comes from the Nyanja language in East Africa: *Little by little, the tortoise arrived at the Indian Ocean.*

Sally Nicholls

1. When I was a creative writing student, we used to have talks from
    lots of agents and editors who would say things like 'Write the story
    that demands to be told!' 'Write the book you can't stop writing!' We
    would all be universally depressed by this, because for us, writing
    was *hard*. We would turn on our computers and spend all day on
    Facebook. We would get stuck. We would wonder if we were good
    enough. The truth is, that quote about genius being 99 per cent
    perspiration and 1 per cent inspiration is true here too. Most of
    the writing life is a coal-face slog. I tell children it's like doing the
    same piece of English homework every day for a year. It is hard.
    It is frustrating. It is even occasionally boring. This is completely
    normal. Sorry.

2. The ability to write a good paragraph is actually fairly common.
    It's also not that difficult. Most of us are not Shakespeare. Don't
    get hung up on writing a beautiful sentence. Pay more attention
    to writing convincing characters living in plausible scenarios and
    dealing with problems and desires that matter a great deal to them
    (and to the reader). Tell a gripping, well-paced story with a satis-
    factory conclusion. That's a lot more important. It's also a hell of a
    lot harder. Sorry about that too.

3. An idea is not the same thing as a plot. *In a hole in the ground lived
    a hobbit* is an idea. *He was unexpectedly employed to rob a dragon* is a
    plot. 'Yer a wizard, Harry!' is an idea. 'And it's down to you to defeat
    Lord Voldemort' is a plot. A novel needs both an idea and a plot.
    However, at its simplest, plot is just 'Someone wants something.
    There is something which will help them to get it. And something
    which will make it difficult. They either succeed or fail.' All stories
    basically boil down to this formula.

4. Don't get too hung up on originality either. The obsession with an original story is actually a comparatively recent phenomenon. 'Boy meets girl' or 'Detective solves crime' are perfectly reasonable plot lines to hang your novel on. Sometimes there's a good reason that gap in the market exists.

5. At the same time, it does make sense to know your market and the genre you want to write in. And to nurture your own sources of inspiration. Read as much as you can, particularly in the genre you're interested in writing. Watch films. Go to the theatre. Watch television. Go to art galleries. Read the absolute best in your field and the absolute bestsellers. And read gripping trash as well.

6. Pay particular attention to the art you love. What do you love about it? The story, the world, the sexy detective? In fact, never stray too far from what you love. Don't try to write what you know. Write what you love. Your enthusiasm will be contagious.

7. One of the most important traits a successful writer possesses is grit. Keep writing even when it's hard (it is hard). Keep submitting even when everyone says 'No' (they will say no). Finish your stories. Send them to every (relevant) agent and publisher in the *Writers' & Artists' Yearbook* if you have to. And get started on the next thing straight away.

8. All writers are very bad at judging their own work. I regularly tell my editor that I think this manuscript 'needs very little editing', only to get pages and pages of feedback. Equally, I'll often submit something saying sheepishly that 'I'm not really happy with it – I know it needs a lot of work', only to be told that it's basically fine. I meet a lot of unpublished writers who have been trying to finish their

first novel for the last ten years. Yes, finishing things is important. As is noticing all the ways they can be improved. But sometimes you just need to grit your teeth, send it out and start the next thing. Or let it go. In general, I'd say if you've been working on something for ten years, it's probably not as 'nearly finished' as you think it is. And the book you should be writing now almost certainly isn't that book any more.

9. Time exists. Most debut writers aren't millionaires or celebrities. They are ordinary people with families and day jobs and stacks of unwashed laundry. I know writers who write on buses. On trains. While their baby sleeps. While their four children watch cartoons. At 5 a.m. I wrote a significant proportion of *Things a Bright Girl Can Do* in a leisure centre cafe surrounded by children on their way to swimming lessons. You have enough time to write. Though you may need to forget about keeping on top of the laundry.

10. Oh … and read your work out loud.

Paraic O'Donnell

1. Start with a strong idea. You know, something compelling, something you just can't get out of your head. Like, what if no one will ever really love you, no matter what you do?

2. Write what you know. Like, maybe you worked as a croupier in Atlantic City, then one time you got suckered into doing a mob hit and the guy had tentacles and turned out to be a fugitive god from another dimension. You didn't? Then fuck you, you're wasting everyone's time.

3. Write every day, even if it's just a few lines. Or you could just draw some lines, you know, or do some colouring in. What's your favourite colour? Your aura is incredible right now, not sure if you're aware. Do you want to get some sushi, maybe?

4. Avoid dream sequences. Readers get impatient with dream sequences, especially if they're in italics. To get around this, make the whole book a dream sequence but don't tell them. In fact, all books are dream sequences, that's the whole fucking point.

5. Use adverbs sparingly. Adverbs are words that modify actions, like 'speedballs' and 'OxyContin'. Ease off the drugs, is what I'm saying. Look at you – what are you, trying to get arrested?

6. Make your characters relatable. Like Diamanda, the Ukrainian agent, she could turn out to be Roxy's twin sister. And Fabio could be the congressman's estranged brother, and therefore – wait for it – a tissue match. Wait, sorry, not relatable. What's the other one again?

7. Always keep a notebook with you. Actually, keep it inside your jacket, and make sure it's thick enough to stop a .32 Parabellum round. In fact, strap Kevlar-covered notebooks to your entire torso and stay away from the windows. OK, now just sit tight. Wait for my call.

8. Never open with weather. I mean, not unless it's really amazing or fucked up weather. Like, if it's raining sharks, that could work. Or if the sun has gone supernova and everyone is on fire, although that's maybe more of an elegiac closing scene.

9. Be careful with period detail. Doing your research is great, but use it sparingly on the page. You can build up atmosphere without mentioning every curio in the fucking antique store.

10. Endings are critical. You've got to resolve everything in a way that feels satisfying, but without making it seem forced or contrived. And no one can do all that, it's just unrealistic. What are you, Megamind? Knock out a few halfway lyrical lines, then have someone walk or turn away. Now go and cash your cheque.

Chibundu Onuzo

1. Don't wait for someone to give you permission to start writing. Lists like this are great, but only if they don't serve as yet another way to procrastinate and put off what you must start today.

2. Drink water. A hydrated writer is the best kind.

3. Nobody writes a novel. People write a chapter if they're lucky. More often they write a page, a paragraph, a sentence, just a word sometimes. Don't be daunted by the task of an entire novel. Take things one sentence at a time.

4. Eat vegetables. Frequent bowel movements also help to expel creative ideas when they are trapped somewhere in your gut.

5. Use your friends and relatives as your first readers. First, because they're free. Secondly, because the average reader of your novel or short story collection is going to be a general reader not a specialist. Some of the most helpful editorial comments I've received are from friends who like reading and can spot what works and what doesn't work in a story.

6. Sleep. Book ideas can come in dreams.

7. Read as widely as you can. Browse the fantasy shelves, as well as the poetry shelves, as well as the science fiction shelves, as well as the literary fiction shelves. Good writing doesn't confine itself to genre.

8. Buy or borrow a copy of the *Writers' & Artists' Yearbook*. This is not a paid advertisement. It's how I found my agent. It also means that when you meet a published writer, you won't need to ask: 'How

did you get an agent?' Instead, a more useful first question will be, 'Is your agent any good?'

9. Don't be put off by rejection letters. As long as you keep writing, no past writing is wasted. It's all part of honing your craft.

10. Stop reading this list and go and write.

Michael Rosen

1. Read, read, read and read.

2. When you read, look out for bits that echo in your head. Collect them. Put them somewhere. Keep them.

3. When you're out and about listen to people. Think about what they say and why they may have said it.

4. When you're talking, if you think you've said something interesting or said something in an interesting way, collect it, put it somewhere, keep it.

5. Never say that you would like to be a writer. Just write.

6. When you write, say the words and phrases and sentences in your head or out loud, listen to the rhythms they make, listen out to make sure that the rhythms match what it is you want to say.

7. What DO you want to say?

8. If you've got nothing to write, it's because you've got nothing to write. That's OK. Do something else.

9. There are thousands of different ways of writing. Don't just try one of them. Try several. Or more than several.

10. After you've written something, try out different ways of reaching people: blogs, joining a writing group, doing a writing course, reading it out loud somewhere, publishing it yourself, video yourself reading it and post it on YouTube, show it to someone you respect, show it to someone you love, show it to someone you hope loves you.

Jacob Ross

Writing is subjective; it is also an expression of personality. We bring our own idiosyncrasies and rituals to the process. Alex Haley and John Cheever dressed in a suit before sitting at a desk to write. For Toni Morrison, a No. 2 pencil and a yellow legal pad were essential tools. Virginia Woolf used a standing desk and Franz Kafka exercised naked in front of his window. If taking a stroll with a lobster on a leash – as Gérard de Nerval allegedly did – is what it takes to kick-start the creative process, then who am I to judge, or advise otherwise?

My teaching and writing comprise a set of 'attitudes and approaches' that may or may not work for some. I hope you find something useful here:

1. Substitute the word *writing* with *storying*. Somehow it modifies the way I approach the work at hand. Storying, in my mind, is the series of circumstances and causally linked incidents and situations that my character experiences as s/he 'journeys' towards the end of the narrative.

2. The essence of characterization is *relationships*. Regardless of how wonderfully a character is described, and however sparkling their dialogue, what drives them is their relationship with themselves, with others and with their world. Much of the writing is about how those relationships are played out on the page, through their desires, their actions and how they respond to what is happening around them. For me, it's been a foolproof method of creating three-dimensional characters, and achieving vivid differentiation between them.

3. Don't 'love-up' your characters to the extent that you don't want to put them in jeopardy. Give them a hard time, make them face

difficult choices, throw obstacles in their path. The American writer Janet Burroway tells us: 'writers are cruel bastards; their job is to give their characters hell'. I live by those words. Characterization is also very much about exploring the extremes that humans are capable of – the sublime as well as the awful. You can, of course, overdo it.

4. Being inhabited by a character/s is no myth. They often take on a life and logic of their own. Don't just allow this to happen, welcome it, and be surprised at what they do and say on the page.

5. The poet Derek Walcott told us that a writer writes 'every day'. That includes *not* writing, because writing also requires thought, rest and 'dreaming' – allowing the subconscious to do part of the work for you. That said, the hardest part of writing is *not* writing, because self-doubt and uncertainty can creep in, and you may even begin to undermine yourself by mistaking this for 'writer's block'.

6. A writer also reads. Reading triggers and feeds the imagination. It shows you strategies and ways of approaching text that you may never have thought of before. The act of reading is as important as that of writing. If you're a 'genre' writer, study the narrative conventions of the form you want to write in, until you understand it well enough to subvert it and impose your own imaginative personality on it. Read like a writer: a reader reads a scene and says it's brilliant; a writer reads that scene and says, it's brilliant, let's see how the author achieved this.

7. A note on understructure. For me, the most challenging part of any book is the beginning. The set-up of any narrative has so much work to do: introduce the world of the story, present the

dominant character/s, assure the reader that they are in good 'storytelling' hands, hint at the 'trouble to come', pull the reader into the narrative (agents and publishers included) and make them want to read on. Those first opening pages are usually what sells the book.

8. I've found that a very useful approach to starting a short- or long-form narrative is holding the 'time' or *temporal axis* foremost in my mind when I begin. Something *has happened* in the past that has consequences for the character/s. Or, something *is happening* that will have consequences. Or, something is *about to happen* that will have consequences. Decide on the *something* that has happened, is happening or is about to happen. This may take anything between a few minutes and a couple of days, if not weeks. It could be as simple as a character deciding to take the stairs rather than the lift, or as overtly devastating as a building falling on a crowd. The key word in all three of the above is *consequences*. Most of the narrative that follows will explore the fallout or consequences of that first event – or, more rarely, series of events – and the way it impacts on a given character, and most likely other characters. Without consequences, there is no story. All there is, is an isolated event that goes nowhere.

9. Escalate, escalate, escalate. One of the really important principles in developing a story is escalation. I've not yet read a good book that does not have escalation as one of its driving principles. Situations get worse and worse, resulting in increasing concern for the 'protagonist' as the story progresses until something gives in the end and there is a 'point of rest' or reprieve. Ignoring that principle can lead to what some editors refer to as 'mid-novel sag'. More often than not, the sag is a deal breaker.

10. Research. Many potentially good works of fiction get flattened by the weight of the research that has been so *obviously* dumped into them. Research is critically important but it should serve the story – not the other way round – and should, in my view, avoid drawing attention to itself. It should be a seamless part of the plot.

And one final item to add to my ten. I like eavesdropping. In fact, I love it. The overheard anecdote, the downright fantastical lies and half-truths that occasionally reach my ears have triggered many a fabulous story idea. It is said that most writers are eavesdroppers, if not shocking gossips. I wish them long life and good health to continue that glorious tradition of listening in when they're supposed to be minding their own business. Good luck and good fortune. Do your best.

Andy Shepherd

I've always dreamt of writing. Ever since I was thirteen years old and wrote my first book, which was so blatantly based on *The Hitchhiker's Guide to the Galaxy* that I had to write to Douglas Adams and apologize for stealing his ideas. (Because I'd never heard of a thing called Fan Fiction.) I still have the reply he sent, wishing me well with my writing. A treasured possession that made me feel part of the 'writer's club' for the first time.

With his words, and the encouragement of a wonderful English teacher, for years I believed I *was* a writer. It was in my blood.

There was just one problem. I stopped writing. And let's be honest, you don't need to be published or win awards to be a writer, but you *do* need to write. I told myself I was too busy with college, too busy with work, too busy with living. Except that wasn't it. Not really. It was fear that stopped me. If I didn't put pen to paper, I could go on telling myself that it was lack of time or the fact I didn't know what to write yet. Rather than facing the fear that what I wrote might not be any good. That *I* wasn't good enough to be part of the 'writer's club'. And so the days turned into years and the empty page turned into many empty pages.

Then one day I started telling stories to my lovely boys. And their eyes lit up and I picked up a pen and started scribbling the stories down, just for the fun of it. And it felt so good that immediately I was transported right back to those endless hours lying on my bedroom carpet, lost in my own words and worlds.

And so I have to thank Douglas Adams once again. Because I knew if I was going to write a book, the time was now. At the auspicious age of forty-two. And this time I was determined to listen to his famous words: 'Don't Panic'. Alongside that piece of wonderful advice, here are a few things I've stumbled across along the way.

1. Start writing and don't stop. Every writer I know has the nagging doubts and critical voices blathering on inside their heads. The trick is to keep writing despite them. These days I usually throw out a few 'Well, I don't see you having a go!' comments to my inner critic. On a practical note, carve out some time and space to actually get the words down. If *you* don't prioritize your writing, it's unlikely anyone else will.

2. Write what you love. You're going to spend a long time with your story and you might not like it every day. But if you love it, you'll stick with it till the end.

3. Find the heart of the story. You need to know why things happen, not just what happens. I always know if I have what I call the 'heart-spark' of a story there, because I'm excited to start writing it. And having that in my mind (and sometimes printed out and stuck to my forehead) helps to keep me on track as the story unfolds.

4. Carve out some space for yourself too, away from the word count. Writing can be fun, but it can also be frustrating and all-consuming. If you don't look after yourself, creativity tends to sulk in a corner.

5. Keep your eyes open for the magic in the world. I love the idea of serendipity. It's like real magic in the everyday. Those moments when ideas suddenly appear to you, or plot threads serenely untangle or a character arrives uninvited. If your eyes aren't open you might just miss them.

6. There will be fallow times. This is OK. Don't Panic.

7. Be patient.

8. Editing is your friend – don't be afraid of it. Just be wise about who you show your work to in the early days. Be protective. Those first words of feedback have the power to lift you up or knock you to the floor if you're not careful. But when you find it, good editorial guidance can be the gift you need in order to take your writing to a whole new level. So embrace it and do the work. It'll be worth it. Having said that, remember to trust yourself too and trust your story. Sometimes only you know what is right.

9. Every book will be different. It doesn't mean you've forgotten how to write. (I have to say this to myself *a lot*.)

10. One last little note, take all advice with a pinch of salt. I got very hung up on the well-worn idea that you must write every day. Because I *couldn't* always write every day. Did that mean I wasn't a writer? Was I not welcome in the 'writer's club', after all? Once I interpreted it as simply meaning 'regularly connect with your writing process in some way', I relaxed. Because I still dream a lot. And dreaming is a huge part of writing.

   It's easy to read 'rules' and feel excluded if you do things differently. But there are as many ways to write as there are writers. All our voices matter. Don't ever feel excluded from the 'writer's club'. If you write, you *are* a writer. However you get the words on the page.

Francesca Simon

I write because I love to read. I love being around books, I love their smell, I love holding them, and I feel happiest in book-filled rooms. I started writing stories not long after I started reading, but I didn't publish fiction until my thirties.

1. I give you permission to write a bad first draft. All first drafts are dreadful. They are always mushy and embarrassing and painful. The trick is to make your second, third and fourth drafts better.

2. Finish what you start. Get to the end even if you skip the middle. Once you have the roughest of drafts you can get to work. Revising is much easier than writing. Don't get stuck in the quicksand of unfinished first drafts. That way madness lies.

3. Set a modest daily word count goal. Mine is 500 words. The reason it's so low is that it means I can never say, 'Oh, I only have a couple of hours, no point in writing today ...'

4. There are no writing rules, other than finishing what you start. You can even write the end first and leave the middle till last. I like to write in the morning, but that's me.

5. Just because you're a writer doesn't mean you can write on any subject whatever. It takes time to find out what you're actually good at writing. If I hadn't had a baby, I would never have discovered that writing for children was my strength.

6. Keep a notebook. I love stationery, and keep a tiny Moleskine notebook with me at all times, as I get ideas when I'm travelling about. However, I only write at my desk in my top-floor office, which brings me to ...

7.   Have a quiet space to write. Even if it's a desk in the corner of the room, make that your writing place.

8.   If you're stuck, move on to a chapter you know you CAN write.

9.   There is no such thing as writer's block. There are tricky problems that may take time to solve. Be confident you will find a solution.

10. Often two ideas which seem unrelated are in fact part of the same story.

Chitra Soundar

1. Tell your unique story. There is someone waiting to hear it.

2. Be true to your story and its characters, not the stereotype you're cast into.

3. Ask for help when you need it – we all need it at some point.

4. Some opportunities don't come until you turn the corner. Take a chance and turn that corner. Say YES.

5. Light your own candles in dark places. Then there will be light wherever you are.

6. Don't fret from the sideline. Join in, beat your drums, make some noise.

7. Always leave trails for those behind you.

8. Remember that there are always more places at the table. You're not taking anyone else's.

9. And a final thought, which is also a way to begin. Like 'once upon a time' in English, in Tamil we used to start stories with 'in a certain place ...' ஒரு ஊரிலே. Have you ever thought what are the conventions in other cultures? I asked this question on Twitter and the response has been incredible. People from all round the world shared their ideas: Once upon a time, long long ago, in the first of times, when tigers smoked pipes and plants and animals could speak, beyond seven mountains and seven rivers, far far away, in a certain place, east of the sun and west of the moon, there was and there wasn't. And thus, the story unfolds.

Colin Thubron

1. Create a writing environment as close to solitude as you can.

2. Don't be afraid of the blank page. Just fill it – even with rubbish. This may stimulate you to correct it – then you write on.

3. Word choice: prefer the Saxon to the Roman.

4. Incorporate adjectives and adverbs into the verb (e.g. 'the jewels glitter on the ground' is stronger than 'the glittering jewels lie on the ground').

5. Don't be inhibited writing a risqué passage. Just write it as if nobody will ever read it (and modify later if you must).

6. No exclamation marks.

7. Leave a gap of time – the longer the better – between finishing a passage and its revision. The cold eye sees clearest.

8. Research in the field: note down the details. It's the details that give a description life.

9. The power of your imagining should eliminate the strain for outward effect.

10. Don't copy other writers. Find your own way. Every rule (including these) can be creatively broken.

Novuyo Rosa Tshuma

1. Believe, against all odds, from whatever obscure corner of the world you are toiling, that what you are doing is worthwhile.

2. Read everything and anything, good, bad, terrible, great. It is good to know what is possible out there, if only to expand and stimulate your own imagination.

3. Inspire yourself daily, be it by reading nuggets from writers you admire, or reading promising paragraphs from your own writing.

4. Be wildly ambitious. Go all out. Ignore all naysayers. They are braying horses soon to be forgotten by history.

5. Do not be in a rush to publish. Once a work is out in the world, it is out there forever. Instead, cultivate discernment in your writing, and produce work you are proud to share.

6. Ignore trends. Fads are just that, soon to be forgotten, as with all imitations. Aim to write work that is original.

7. Measuring yourself against the carefully curated fictions of writers on social media will only make you feel bad about your writing and suck away your precious writing time.

8. Avoid cliques and the plague of group-thinking. Hanging around other writers does not make you a writer. Protect yourself and your work, surrounding yourself with fellow scribes of mutual understanding, talents and ambitions.

9. To be a writer, you must write. TO BE A WRITER, YOU MUST WRITE. To be a great writer, you must write well.

10. Put in the hours. Put in the work. Believe enough in the beauty and the importance of what you're doing to want to do it well.

10.1. 'Your train is never late. It's always on time.' Words of wisdom I carry everywhere I go, from my friend and fellow writer Marcus Burke.

Irvine Welsh

1. Do it. Don't think about it. Composition is about action and only tangentially about thought.

2. Do it anywhere. Writing, like sex, should not be confined to one space.

3. Finish the story before reading it. Don't rewrite or even re-read till you've finished the first draft. A story has a beginning, middle and end.

4. Don't show early drafts to anybody. If you are doing your job properly they will look a mess. They are supposed to. They are solely there for you to make them into something readable.

5. Know yourself. Do you like spending a lot of time on your own? If not then trying to be a writer will only frustrate you.

6. Read a lot between writing.

7. Have a lot of music on when you write the early drafts. They are better with stimulus.

8. Have total silence when you write the later drafts. This is about craft and concentration.

9. If you aren't getting anywhere put it in a drawer and write about something else. Then go back to it in a couple of weeks with a clear head.

10. Disregard all of the above and find something that works for you.

Adam Weymouth

1. I grew up reading Kerouac, and assumed that my best writing would come in divine floods of inspiration, probably substance-induced, probably very late at night. Invariably, that's not the case. Much to the shame of my former teenage self, I do my best writing mid-morning. Waiting for inspiration is an extremely protracted way to write a book. I have found out since that secretly Kerouac grafted pretty hard as well.

2. Share your work. Now, today, before it's perfect. Start a writers' circle if there isn't one nearby. Until you can get over your fear of exposing your work in public, and come to understand that any failings in your writing say nothing whatsoever about your worth as a human being, you will be impossibly hampered.

3. Close the door. Shut everyone out when you work. That includes closing the door on the internet. If you don't have the discipline for that (I don't) then there are apps that will temporarily cut your connection.

4. That doesn't mean you must work in isolation. Writing is an odd way to spend one's time. Frequently I don't have my first conversation until the evening. I like to work in libraries, for a sense of solidarity and company with compatriots.

5. I write first drafts in pencil. My mind works in a different way by hand.

6. Get down the details in the moment. I carry a notebook with me, always, and will write when I am face to face with my subject (again, in pencil). I think of it like sketching. If I cannot write in the moment, I write *as soon as possible* after the fact. The richest details

have an incredibly short half-life. There is time later for refinement, but it is often the images and phrases that I get down when I am there that become the most vivid parts of a passage. Notebooks with waterproof pages are available for canoe trips.

7. Apply for grants and residencies. They are wonderful ways to focus on your work away from the daily frets of life and money.

8. I learnt to write when I walked to Istanbul. I didn't take anyone with me, but I did take a lot of notebooks, and I wrote in them for hours every night. It was my time to experiment, an apprenticeship, to learn without structure or deadline. I came to think of writing as a way to inhabit the world more deeply. I have always believed that living comes first. Writing is a way of better understanding living.

9. I'm afraid I can't see the point in travel or nature writing without a social or environmental conscience.

10. To be handed someone's story should be a reciprocal process. Consider how your work can give back to them.

BEGINNING

BEAUTIFUL PLANET
Neal Layton

↑

EARTH
(WHERE WE ALL LIVE)

4 STEPS

TO BEING ~~CREATIVE~~ CREATIVE

AND SHARING COOL IDEAS
WHILST ALSO HELPING THE
PLANET...

① GET SOME PAPER

PAPER HAS BEEN USED TO SHARE IDEAS FOR THOUSANDS OF YEARS...
(LIKE THE EGYPTIANS AND THIS BOOK)
BUT PAPER IS MADE FROM PLANTS SO WE NEED TO **VALUE** IT.
HERE ARE SOME IDEAS...

- USE ETHICALLY SOURCED PAPER

- USE OLD PAPER, LIKE THE BACKS OF boring computer print outs.
- OR THE INSIDES OF CEREAL PACKETS, OR BROWN PAPER BOXES

- AND IF YOU DO HAPPEN TO DO A RUBBISH DRAWING, OR SPELL SOMETHING RONG RECYCLE IT!

② GET SOME PENCILS

PENCILS ARE AMAZING!

YOU CAN WRITE WITH THEM, DRAW WITH THEM. PRESS HARD AND GET **DARK** MARKS, LIGHTER FOR LIGHT MARKS.

YOU CAN USE THEM UPSIDE DOWN, AND IN SPACE

THEY BIO DEGRADE SO THERE IS NO WASTE.

SOME IDEAS..
- BUY ETHICALLY SOURCED PENCILS
- TRY DIFFERENT WEIGHTS
- TRY MAKING DIFFERENT MARKS,

~~SEE EVERY~~

- PENCILS COME FROM TREES AND GRAPHITE (WHICH IS MINED)

SO MAKE SURE YOU USE EVERY LAST BIT

③ GET SOME INK!

INK IS AMAZING

GET A REFILLABLE FOUNTAIN PEN,

OR A DIP PEN

OR A STICK OR A

BRUSH...

TRY WRITING AND

DRAWING AND

MAKING EXPRESSIVE

MARKS...

REUSABLE

INK

← RECYCLABLE

USING OF [INK] IN A GLASS BOTTLE IS LESS
WASTEFUL THAN DISPOSABLE PENS

⊕ AND FINALLY GET SOME

IDEAS OR AND WRITE, DRAW OR DESIGN

THEM!! FINDING

IDEAS TO SHARE shouldn't

BE DIFFICULT WHEN YOU LIVE ON THE MOST **BEAUTIFUL PLANET** IN THE COSMOS.

LET'S DO EVERYTHNG

WE CAN TO KEEP IT THAT WAY.

YEAH!

FORGET THE ODDS
Andy Stanton

Forget who else is doing well, selling a gazillion, getting film deals, commanding a huge fan base ... You've got a job to do, so get back to work and start that next chapter. Stop reading your reviews, because sooner or later you'll read one that haunts you like Marley's ghost and you'll wake up in the middle of the night in a cold sweat and all will seem doomed, and I mean, what's even wrong with you, it was a 4-star review for goodness' sake; but all you can think about is that one missing star, that missing, un-coloured-in star that spins through your dreams like a transparent grinning demon, proclaiming your many and irreparable failings to the world.

Don't let success go to your head or disappointment defeat you. Believe in the worth of your work but don't make the mistake of thinking you're Someone Important, that's just embarrassing. Stay honest and give back to the writing community: mentor an aspiring writer, add your voice to a campaign against library closures, waive an appearance fee for a deserving cause. It's essential that you don't come to see your every creative thought as saleable or you'll lose the sense of playfulness that started you writing in the first place.

Be extraordinarily exacting in your work. Weigh every word, interrogate every resonance to ensure you're saying what you think you want to say. At the same time, avoid the curse of perfectionism, which leads to second-guessing and paralysis and entire weeks/months/years lost to moping and daytime TV.

Exceed people's expectations whenever you can. Spend just a little too long with each fan in your book queue: talk to them and listen to them and take them seriously, and remember you're lucky to have them. (Secret Machiavellian bonus: this also has the effect of making your signing queue last significantly longer, which will greatly annoy and unnerve the other authors signing at nearby tables, especially if you're new to the scene and they're all wondering just who the hell *is* this disconcertingly popular upstart, anyway. I said you shouldn't worry about the competition – but you've got to be a bit of a trickster from time to time or where's the fun?)

Curb your self-promotion. Let people know you've got new stuff out there, but don't re-tweet your good reviews (why are you even still reading your reviews, by the way?) or constantly bombard the world with your success. It's smug and needy and unseemly, and besides, there are lots of other things going on in the world that are infinitely more important than a photo of you yukking it up in the green room. (You're allowed a *few* of these a year. A very few.) Have some confidence that your work is good enough to find its audience without constant shepherding and insistence on your part.

Be nice. Be humble. Be generous. Forget the odds and forget the potential rewards. Write well, try hard and let the rest take care of itself.

FESTIVAL QUESTIONS
Simon Garfield

Some questions I've been asked at book festivals that I have a better answer to now than I did then ...

1. *Where do you get your ideas from?* Some come from editors who know my interests/obsessions/limitations, and some spend a year or two festering in my brain, perhaps inspired by a newspaper article or book. Post-fester, they come out for a two-month research period, and if they still hold up after that they may form the basis for a proper long-term project. All my other ideas I pick up on the way home from Marks & Spencer.

2. *How do you choose your titles?* I've always been averse to even the mildest of puns. However, three of my biggest sellers have been *Just My Type*, *On the Map* and *To the Letter*, so there. My only advice is to find an editor who's good at these things and trust them. That said, the initial suggestion for my fonts book was *Not My Type*, but I accentuated the positive.

3. *Do you have a set pattern to the writing day?* The only constant is morning coffee. I tend to be more particular about that than I do about the method of writing (laptop/iPad/paper all fine) or the venue (kitchen/cafe/library also all fine). I don't set a daily word target, as so much depends on the subject matter. If I'm writing up an interview I can easily manage 2,000 words, but if there's a tricky bit of theorizing 400 will do. And as we all know, it's the rewriting that counts. This will appear preposterous no doubt, but I tend to work best between 4 and 4.30 p.m. If I'm

working at 4.30 then it's a sign that the writing is in full swing, and I haven't packed in for the day/given in to a sugar low/gone to a movie. If I'm working between 4 and 4.30 p.m. I may still be working at 8.30 p.m., which is always good news (for the book, if not my family).

4. *Do you read or care about your reviews?* Yes I care, and no I tend not to read them. Critics perform a crucial service, and I love reading book reviews (and occasionally write them). I love good criticism from editors and readers before publication, but I'm not sure how much it helps me after publication. If the reviews are good I get sent them by my agent and publisher, and if they're 'mixed' they tend to keep quiet, so I always have a fair idea about how a book's been received. And almost every time there are some raves, some pans, and some in-between. The same with reviews online. My favourite reviews on Amazon are the ones that say, '5 Stars: the book arrived promptly and in perfect condition, and I'm sure my uncle will love it.' But the best review I ever got was from Stuart Shorter in the book *Stuart: A Life Backwards* by Alexander Masters. He saw my book *Mauve* on Alexander's shelf, and, after finding out that it was indeed about the colour mauve, commented 'How'd he fucking get away with it?'

5. *What's the worst public literary event you've ever done?* Most authors will have stories about not many people turning up to a reading in a bookshop because it was snowing/transport wasn't working/no one was at all interested in the book, and some authors will have stories about doing a great talk for a big crowd and then the book not being there to sign afterwards. But I also have this. The last talk I did (a few weeks ago) was at

something called the Boring Conference, where a lot of nerdy types gather to hear equally nerdy people talk about things that are obscure but actually fascinating, such as the paper clip. I was the final speaker of the day, clearly saving the best till last, and about an hour before I was due on I went for a walk, tripped and fell, and broke a couple of ribs. But being the Total Pro, I went on as if nothing had happened. Not a good move. I was clearly still in shock, couldn't remember anything about my subject, barely knew who or where I was, and just rambled away. I could see the audience looking glazed, but I just carried on regardless. Definitely the most boring talk of the day. So if this is being read by aspiring authors looking for useful advice, I'd advise against doing that.

WELL-WORN PHRASES
Tracy Chevalier

How has it happened that I've managed to do something many others haven't? I've written and published ten novels so far and am able to make a living from my writing. Aspiring writers often ask me what the key to this productivity is, thinking there is something they don't know or haven't heard of. I suspect they secretly hope I will give them a vial of fairy dust they can sprinkle around and – *voilá*! – out comes a fully formed novel. Unfortunately, I'm about to repeat things everyone else has said. Indeed, they can be summed up in three well-worn phrases, which I'm going to briefly unpack to explain the Why behind the What:

1. *Writing is 1 per cent inspiration and 99 per cent perspiration.* (Thank you, Thomas Edison.) When I read a novel, I like it to run inevitably forward on a track, with the sense that the writer is just a few pages ahead of me, pulling me along as the ink flows. In order to get that feeling of flow, a writer needs to get in the zone and *stay* in the zone. Once you start, you have to keep going. If you set aside the writing for two months, the reader will feel that gap. So, persistence. You may not feel like writing today – and indeed, 99 per cent of the time I really don't feel inspired. But you have to do it anyway, inspired or not. It's your job. I've often found that even when I'm not inspired, I'm perfectly capable of crafting a good sentence, a good scene, a surprising character trait. It's not about inspiration – or not just about inspiration; it really is about putting the time in, in a consistent way.

2. *Form follows function.* (Thank you, Louis Sullivan.) I think this is the thing that trips up writers the most. Often someone will have a great story idea but the writing lets it down by not adding to it in any way. This is the case with many published books. Or, less common but it still happens, a writer is in love with words and phrases and writes beautiful things that mean nothing. This happens a lot in poetry. On rare, magical occasions, the writing doesn't just support the story, it enhances it. The two get bound up in each other and become inextricable. In other words, what you say and how you say it should go hand in hand. Example: when I wrote *Girl with a Pearl Earring* I decided to write in the style of a Vermeer painting – spare, focused, understated – since that was what the novel was about. If I had written in big, overblown prose – Rubens rather than Vermeer – the book would have been completely different, and wouldn't have worked.

3. *The only kind of writing is rewriting.* (Thank you, Ernest Hemingway.) If you write a sentence and think, 'Wow, that is great, I'm not going to touch it' – it probably isn't great, and needs touching. You have to question everything, and be your own worst critic. Each word you write has to be justified; it has to work for its place on the page. If you don't question it, but leave it to someone else (an editor? an intrepid friend?), you're shirking your duty. The thing about rewriting is that actually it's easier than writing. At least there is something – no matter how bad – to work on. Nothing is scarier than a blank page, not even bad prose.

There are many other things I could say about writing, but you will have heard them. Now, you just have to go and *do it.*

ABOUT TO BE
Isabelle Dupuy

There are no writers in paradise. I'm a firm believer in necessity as the mother of invention. I, for example, have a fear of abandonment that has fuelled my creativity. I started by living the plots and dramas I would write. Live one-liners and record comebacks landed hot on the page, never quite as raw and uncensored as one would have hoped. It's the Hemingway model: turn your life into a work of fiction and report on it. Most of us try this at one point or another. It's not a good survival strategy because it's exhausting, and more importantly, it implies that you don't respect your own life. This has a way of catching up with you.

You may be motivated, as Orwell wrote, by revenge if you feel powerless or a need to be heard in your own voice. Nora Ephron said 'everything is copy'. Tragedy plus time equals Comedy. This too shall pass unless you write it down and once you do, you've taken control of that history. It's as much about writing as it is about coping. That's the only power I ever found in my wars against pain. 'What are you trying to say?' is a question I ask myself every day. The aim is not art, it is always life. Writing gives sense to mine.

To write you need time. You can produce pages that say nothing. You can write for years and remain in the darkest obscurity. Go on. My first novel is about to be published. I'm still closer to the aspiring novelist than the acclaimed author. Opportunity cost still bites. I watched friends and family move up in their careers, saw London move and evolve around me while I deleted rejection emails. I started writing this novel before the word Brexit existed. Before the musical *Hamilton* was first performed off-Broadway, before the documentary series *Planet Earth* and the new wing at Tate Modern. As a woman who's emigrated twice – the first time when I was eighteen from Haiti to America, the second time, ten years later, from New York to London – I'm used to fear dilution; that my bits of life in each country disqualified me from owning an identity from which to create from. What I really needed was permission.

Once that happened, writing opened connections, across oceans, across time to people and places I never knew mattered. Clues to the mystery of how we come to be. Read before you write to establish your place in the chain of human thought. And then write with compassion for yourself and you will access the heart of all your characters.

BANISH THE DARK
Thomas Keneally

First, let me praise the writing process which has saved me from being a derelict and a fringe-dweller. To write is to be, even at eighty-three years of age, perpetually young. It is the same process for all of us, whether we're twenty-one or ninety. It is ageless in its challenges and excitements. At the risk of sounding pietistic, it is my daily bread and my salvation.

There may be writers who know exactly where they are going with a novel from the beginning. The rest of us begin in bewilderment, but driven by the obscure necessity to start, we feel our way through the first draft and to a conclusion. I think writing a novel is like a journey undertaken say by the Polynesians who in the thirteenth or fourteenth century discovered and settled New Zealand. They had heard rumour of land there, they knew the stars to steer by and their general bearing, but as they set out with their cast of character-rowers they did not know for certain what Behemoths, what islands, what strangers, what tempests they would encounter. Like them, we are not fully in charge of our material as we write the early version of our novel; we discover what the book is by writing it. The relentless paddling reveals all.

And that is because our un-conscious mind, the part of our mind (Jung's collective unconscious perhaps) where the gods and all the avatars, all vision, all rites of passage, all journeys, all tests, all ironies are stored, begins to work on our simple structure, or primitive narrative, almost without our knowing it. We might only write two to eight hours a day, but the unconscious mind works on our plot and characters, on the sinews and potential subtleties of the book, twenty-four hours a day – yes, even in sleep. That is why the cry is, 'Only Begin!' Begin with your humble and ordinary conscious brain, which is probably fancier than mine, and find out from your un-conscious mind the things you did not know you knew, the organic connections between all the elements of what you write.

That's the thing: outsiders see the novel as an exercise in control, but if you find as you hack your way in by the 1,000, or just 500, words at a time, that you don't quite know where you're going and you feel hapless – that's the price of writing a novel. Accept it, and don't take it too seriously. To be bewildered is fine, as long as you still write.

Another image: to write a novel is to enter a dark room. There are people in there – you can see dim outlines. Some of them love each other, others are primed to do ridiculous things in love's name, others are stricken with inconvenient and dramatic visions, and others want to kill each other. The more you talk to them, through what you write, the more the lights come on, the more the features are defined and the vividness of character flashes in their eyes.

For beginners: there are no rules, or if there are Dostoevsky and Hemingway and Toni Morrison and all your favourite novelists have broken them. If there is a rule, then it is this: if you wonder whether you need another writing class or not, begin writing. We come back to: Only Begin! You cannot begin too early and you cannot write enough. If you write a sort of letter each day to your novel, even if the letter is to say you don't know where to go next, you will be astounded at the mass of material you possess after six months, and the smoothing and connecting work your various forms of intelligence, conscious and unconscious, have done on it.

So if you can think of nothing to write, write yourself or someone you love a letter about how you are stuck (see John McPhee's wonderful *Draft No. 4*, the best book I have seen on writing). Enumerate what your objectives are, and go through the options you have to advance the book, options you think are too trite, too predictable, too creaky. Write them anyhow. Write dialogue to go with the scenes, and write about the architecture or weather of a scene. By the time you have been through all your choices it is very likely that the solution will have presented itself – you may indeed have given yourself a few unexpected chapters. For writing itself is always a revelation.

If you feel unworthy of the task, join the club. It's quite a club. It includes Dickens and George Eliot. And remember who they are: people from the edges of life, the place the good novelists come from. So if you ask yourself, what right has a person like yourself to presume to write a novel, that is the beginning of writing wisdom and is your warrant to start.

TELLING STORIES
Huw Lewis-Jones

One of the first stories I remember writing was about a boy who entered a raffle and won a trip to the North Pole. My teacher put it in a contest and it scraped a prize. The result: a proud mum, a slightly bewildered seven year old and a certificate blu-tacked to my door for a few weeks before football posters took over again. Almost thirty years later I reached the North Pole for real, voyaging on a ship as a historian. Telling stories. I finally managed to be there. *Patience pays.*

As a writer, and a teacher, I travel to remote places and also spend a lot of time in my chair. Drinking in the world around me and finding inspiration each day with books and the people I meet. I enjoy encouraging others in their own creating. I try to open their minds to new ideas, even if it is just the smallest thing. And it doesn't stop me bumbling along with something else. As Ray Bradbury said: *I stuff my eyes with wonder.*

Writers of all types do things their own way. There is plenty of contradictory advice in this gathering of golden rules – is that so surprising? Each writer is telling their story the way it is, or has been, for them. Your own way will be your way, and your story yours to write the way you want it.

But all the writers here are also sharing much of the same advice: try to keep yourself happy, healthy and *get on with it.* They are all professional in what they are doing. Committed to turn up to work, to honour the promise they made to themselves – to try to add to what they wrote the day before, and to see it to completion. I try to create something every day, no matter how small it might seem, because all the little things soon come together. Even the writing of a list can be a surprisingly creative act.

Life is a journey, full of stories, and everyone is free to invent their own. That's a cliché, of course, but most clichés are true. The more you stop to look and listen, the more you will see, and the more you will write. Most good fiction is a case of taking what is already out there and giving it a new life, a new shape.

Writing is tough. Why do it? Because you like it and you know you can become better at it, even though it often causes unhappiness and anxiety. Remember, no one is forcing you to write. So get back inside the whale and stop complaining.

There's plenty going on today that should be a cause for concern. The climate is in crisis, children are suffering and the forests are burning. There are far more important things to be worried about in the world than worrying about writing. But thinking about books and finding ways to bring others happiness is not indulgent. That's what the best writers do. They have the power to bring joy into the world.

Let's not begin to imagine a world without books. That's too sad for words. Stop, look and listen, remember. We still have the chance to write a different final paragraph. Imagine a new tomorrow. Pick up a different book, re-read a favourite. Listen to the wisdoms you'll find on the page. Today I chose T. H. White's *The Sword in the Stone* and heard Merlin speaking to the young King Arthur. 'The best thing for being sad is to learn something', says Merlin. 'That's the only thing that never fails.'

Biographies

Author-editor
HUW LEWIS-JONES is an award-winning author and a seafarer, with a PhD from the University of Cambridge. He is now Senior Lecturer at Falmouth University, where he encourages his students that it's usually better to be outside than in. Published in sixteen languages, his books include *The Sea Journal*, *Explorers' Sketchbooks*, *Imagining the Arctic*, *Archipelago*, *The Conquest of Everest*, which won the History Award at the Banff Festival, and *The Writer's Map*, a bestselling atlas of imaginary lands. When not writing Huw escapes into wilderness areas as a naturalist and expedition leader and has been twelve times to the North Pole.

Contributors
KWAME ALEXANDER is a poet, educator and the *New York Times* bestselling author of thirty-three books, including *The Undefeated*, illustrated by Kadir Nelson, *Swing*, *Rebound*, which was shortlisted for the prestigious Carnegie Medal, and his Newbery medal-winning middle-grade novel, *The Crossover*. He is the inaugural Innovator-in-Residence at The American School in London.

JIM AL-KHALILI is an academic scientist, author and broadcaster based at the University of Surrey, where he holds a Distinguished Chair in quantum physics. He is the author of twelve books, translated into over twenty languages – including his first novel, *Sunfall*. He is also a regular presenter of TV science documentaries and is probably best known as the host of the long-running weekly BBC Radio 4 programme, *The Life Scientific*. He is a recipient of the Royal Society Michael Faraday medal, the Institute of Physics Kelvin Medal and the inaugural Stephen Hawking Medal for Science Communication.

DAVID ALMOND is the author of *Skellig*, *The Dam*, *The Colour of the Sun* and many other novels, stories, picture books, songs, opera libretti and plays. His work is translated into forty languages, and is widely adapted for stage and screen. His most recent book is *Joe Quinn's Poltergeist*, a graphic novel with Dave McKean. His major awards include the Carnegie Medal and the Hans Christian Andersen Award, the world's most prestigious prize for children's authors. He is Professor of Creative Writing at Bath Spa University and lives in Newcastle upon Tyne.

SOPHIE ANDERSON's debut novel, *The House with Chicken Legs*, was short-listed for the CILIP Carnegie Medal, Waterstones Children's Book Prize, Blue Peter Book Award, British Book Awards Children's Fiction Book of the Year and Branford Boase Award. Her second novel is *The Girl Who Speaks Bear*. Sophie lives in the Lake District with her husband and their four children.

PHILIP ARDAGH is an award-winning children's author of more than 100 books, translated into over forty languages. His prizes include the Roald Dahl Funny Prize and Germany's prestigious Deutscher Jugendliteraturpreis. He regularly turns up on radio and TV, talking books. *The Independent* described him as 'a national treasure' and he was Beard of Summer in 2018.

YABA BADOE is a Ghanaian-British filmmaker and writer. A graduate of King's College, Cambridge, she was a civil servant in Ghana before becoming a general trainee with the BBC. She has taught in Spain and Jamaica, and worked at the University of Ghana. Her short stories have been published in *Critical Quarterly*, *African Love Stories* and *Daughters of Africa*. Her first adult novel, *True Murder*, was published by Jonathan Cape in 2009; her first YA novel, *A Jigsaw of Fire and Stars*, was shortlisted for the Branford Boase Award in 2018 and nominated for the CILIP Carnegie Award 2018. *Wolf Light* was published in 2019. Yaba lives in London.

HARRY BAKER is a World Poetry Slam Champion and published his debut anthology, *The Sunshine Kid*, in 2014. The show of the same name was voted 'Best Spoken Word Show' of the Edinburgh Fringe Festival 2015. Now a fully fledged maths graduate and full-time poet, his work has been shared on TED.com and viewed millions of times worldwide, as well as being trans-lated into twenty-one languages. He is currently working on a show around maths and poetry as he has just turned 10,000 days old. He lives in Margate

ALEX BELL is the author of ten novels for children and young people. She wrote her first published book when she was nineteen and studying Law at university. Since then, her work has included the Zoella Book Club choice *Frozen Charlotte*, as well as Waterstones Children's Book of the Month, *The Polar Bear Explorers' Club*.

SITA BRAHMACHARI is an award-winning writer of poems, plays, short stories and novels whose creative community-based projects are at the heart of her work. She has been Writer in Residence for The Book Trust and

Islington Centre for Refugees and Migrants and is an Amnesty Ambassador. She co-created a play inspired by Shaun Tan's novel *The Arrival*. Her celebrated novels include *Artichoke Hearts*, *Jasmine Skies*, *Tender Earth*, *Red Leaves*, *Kite Spirit*, *Worry Angels*, *Brace Mouth*, *False Teeth*, *Car Wash Wish*, *Zebra Crossing Soul Song*, *Corey's Rock* and *Where the River Runs Gold*. She is the recipient of the Waterstones Book Prize and UK Honour for Writing from The International Board of Books for Young People. She lives in London.

ANTHONY BROWNE is an acclaimed author and illustrator with fifty-one titles to his name, including prize-winning bestsellers such as *Gorilla* (winner of the Kate Greenaway Medal and the Kurt Maschler Award), *Willy the Wimp*, *My Dad*, *Voices in the Park* (winner of Kurt Maschler Award) and *Zoo* (winner of the Kate Greenaway Medal). In 2009 he was appointed Children's Laureate, in recognition of his outstanding contribution to the world of picture books. He was also the first British winner of the Hans Christian Andersen Award, one of the highest international honours for illustration. His work has been widely exhibited and his books are published all over the world. He lives in Kent.

EDWARD CAREY is a writer and illustrator whose books include *The Iremonger Trilogy*, *Observatory Mansions* and *Alva & Irva: The Twins Who Saved a City*. His artwork has been exhibited in Britain, Ireland, Italy and America; his essays and reviews have been published in the *New York Times*, *Guardian*, *Observer*, *Corriere della Serra* and *La Repubblica*. His most recent book, *Little*, is a fictionalized autobiography of the early life of Madame Tussaud. His latest novel, *Fish House*, is about the two years that Geppetto spent inside a whale. He is currently working on his eighth book, probably about a hospital filled with monsters.

TRACY CHEVALIER is the author of ten novels, including *A Single Thread*, *Remarkable Creatures* and the international bestseller *Girl with a Pearl Earring*, which has sold over five million copies, been translated into forty-three languages and made into an Oscar-nominated film. She is a Trustee of the British Library and has used it to research all of her books. She grew up in Washington, DC, but since 1984 has lived in London.

FRANK COTTRELL-BOYCE is an acclaimed author whose varied career includes bestselling books and successful screenplays, writing episodes for *Coronation Street* and even scripting an Olympics opening ceremony. In 2004, he wrote a book for children based on his own screenplay – *Millions* – which won the 2004 Carnegie Medal; it was published as a play in 2010. His second children's novel, *Framed*, was shortlisted for both the Carnegie Medal and the Whitbread Children's Book of the Year Award. Recent books include *The Unforgotten Coat, Chitty Chitty Bang Bang Flies Again, The Astounding Broccoli Boy* and *Sputnik's Guide to Life on Earth*, which was shortlisted for the Carnegie Medal. He lives in Liverpool.

CRESSIDA COWELL grew up in London and on a small uninhabited island off the west coast of Scotland. She was convinced that there were dragons living on this island, and has been fascinated with them ever since. She studied English Literature at Oxford University and Illustration at St Martin's School of Art and Brighton University. She is well known for her bestselling *How to Train Your Dragon* series of twelve books, now published in thirty-eight languages and transformed into two Oscar-nominated DreamWorks Animation feature films, with the final instalment in the franchise trilogy released in 2019. She has now completed the first three books in a new adventure series, *The Wizards of Once*, a world of wizards, warriors, giants and sprites. In 2019 she was made the Waterstones Children's Laureate.

ISABELLE DUPUY is a new writer. Her first novel *Living the Dream* was published by Jacaranda Books in 2019. She is currently working on her second novel, *The Most Beautiful Woman in Haiti*. She moved to the UK as an investment banker and has lived many lives in London since.

INUA ELLAMS is a cross art form practitioner, a poet, playwright and performer, graphic artist and designer and founder of the Midnight Run – an international, arts-filled, night-time, playful, urban, walking experience. He was born in Nigeria. Across his work, identity, displacement and destiny are reoccurring themes, in which he also tries to mix the old with the new: traditional African storytelling with contemporary poetry, pencil with pixel, texture with vector images. His poetry is published by Flipped Eye, Akashic, Nine Arches, and several plays by Oberon.

MAZ EVANS is an author, scriptwriter and lyricist whose bestselling *Who Let the Gods Out?* series has sold to eighteen countries worldwide and garnered twenty award nominations, including the Carnegie Medal, the Branford Boase and the Waterstones Children's Book Prize. Her acclaimed creative writing events have featured at the Hay, Edinburgh, Cheltenham,

Bath, Imagine, Wilderness and many international festivals. She lives in Dorset with her children, a stationery habit and a sneaking suspicion that one day someone will unmask her for the fraud she really is.

SIMON GARFIELD is the author of nineteen books of non-fiction, including the bestsellers *Mauve*, *Just My Type* and *On the Map*. His study of Aids in Britain, *The End of Innocence*, won the Somerset Maugham Prize. He is a trustee of the Mass Observation Archive and the editor of several books of diaries, including *Our Hidden Lives* and *A Notable Woman*. For more than thirty years his work has appeared in the *Guardian*, *Independent*, *Observer*, *Esquire* and *Granta*, where his subjects have included health issues, technology and popular culture. His latest book is a history of our relationship with dogs.

TOM GAULD is an award-winning illustrator and author of the Eisner-nominated graphic novels *Goliath* and *Mooncop*. For the last decade he has drawn weekly comic strips for the *Guardian*. His first collection, *You're All Just Jealous of My Jetpack*, won the MoCCA Gold Medal and his next, *Baking with Kafka*, won the Eisner Award for best Humour Publication in 2018. He lives in London.

LEV GROSSMAN is the author of five novels including the No. 1 *New York Times* bestselling *Magicians* trilogy, which has been published in twenty-five countries and adapted for television. He spent fifteen years as the book critic and lead technology writer for *Time* magazine and has also written essays and criticism for the *New York Times*, *Salon*, *Slate*, *Wired*, *Vanity Fair*, *The Believer* and the *Wall Street Journal*, among many others. A graduate of Harvard and Yale, he lives in Brooklyn with his wife and three children.

MATT HAIG is the bestselling author of books for adults and children. *Reasons to Stay Alive* spent a year in the *Sunday Times* bestseller list and its follow up, *Notes on a Nervous Planet*, also reached number one and was translated into forty languages. He has written novels for adults including the bestsellers *How to Stop Time*, *The Humans* and *The Radleys*. He has also written a variety of children's novels such as *The Truth Pixie* and *A Boy Called Christmas*, which is being made into a film by the makers of *Paddington* starring Jim Broadbent, Maggie Smith, Sally Hawkins and Kristen Wiig.

VASHTI HARDY is the author of middle-grade fantasy adventures including *Brightstorm*, *Wildspark* and *Darkwhispers*. Her adventure stories have been translated into several languages, selected for Independent Booksellers' Children's Book of the Season and Primary School Book Club Reads, won the West Sussex Children's Story Book Award and shortlisted for the Waterstones Children's Book Prize, Books are My Bag Awards and Leeds Book Award. She lives in West Sussex with her husband and three children.

JOANNE HARRIS is the author of fifteen novels, including *Runemarks*, *The Gospel of Loki* and the award-winning *Chocolat*, which was adapted into a BAFTA- and Oscar-nominated film. Since *Chocolat* all her books have been UK bestsellers, ranging widely from French cookbooks to Norse mythology, short stories to dark thrillers, and she has also been on the judging panels of numerous literary competitions, including the Whitbread Book Awards and the Orange Prize for Fiction. Her books are published in over fifty countries. She was formerly a teacher of modern languages.

MICHELLE HARRISON is the author of seven novels for children and young adults, and her books have been translated into eighteen languages. Her first, *The Thirteen Treasures*, won the Waterstones Children's Book Prize. *The Other Alice* won the Calderdale Book of the Year Award. Prior to being a full-time writer, she worked as a bookseller and then as an editor for Oxford University Press. She lives in Essex and has a son called Jack and three cats.

PHILIP HOARE is the author of eight works of non-fiction, and is very fond of whales.

A.M. HOMES is an author, teacher and television executive-producer. Her novels include *This Book Will Save Your Life*, which won the Women's Prize for Fiction in 2013, *Music for Torching*, *The End of Alice* and *Jack*. She has also written the short-story collections *Days of Awe* and *The Safety of Objects*, as well as an acclaimed memoir, *The Mistress's Daughter*. Her work has been translated into twenty-two languages and appears frequently in journals such as *Granta* and *The New Yorker*. She is currently developing a new television project with BBC America, teaches in the Creative Writing Program at Princeton University and lives in New York City.

NADINE AISHA JASSAT is an award-winning poet, writer and creative practitioner. Her debut poetry collection, *Let Me Tell You This*, was shortlisted for a Scottish Herald Arts and Culture Award for Outstanding Literature. Her non-fiction features in *It's Not About the Burqa* and *Nasty Women*, and her fiction and poetry have drawn acclaim: in 2018 she won a Scottish Book Trust New Writers' Award for Fiction and the British Council's UK Open Call for the *Discover* project, as well as being shortlisted for the Outspoken London Prize for Poetry in Film and the prestigious Edwin Morgan Poetry Award. She was named one of 30 Inspiring Women Under 30 in Scotland, where she lives and works.

CARSTEN JENSEN was born in 1952 on the island of Ærø in the Baltic, the son of a sailor. He has written twenty-five books, among them the travelogue *I Have Seen the World Begin* and the novels *We, the Drowned* and *The First Stone*. He lives in Copenhagen.

CATHERINE JOHNSON has written over twenty books for young readers, including *Sawbones*, *The Curious Tale of the Lady Caraboo* and *Freedom*, an IBBY Honour list book for 2020, and winner of the Little Rebel Award. She has written for film, including *Bullet Boy*, and for television and radio. She lives by the seaside.

THOMAS KENEALLY was born in 1935 and his first novel was published in 1964. Since then he has written close to sixty novels and non-fiction works. His novels include *The Chant of Jimmie Blacksmith*, *Schindler's List*, *The People's Train*, *Daughters of Mars*, *Napoleon's Last Island* and most recently *Crimes of the Father*. His history books include *The Great Shame*, *Australians* and *The Commonwealth of Thieves*. He has won numerous awards including the Booker Prize, the Miles Franklin Award, the *Los Angeles Times* Prize and the Mondello International Prize, and has been made a Literary Lion of the New York Public Library. He is recipient of the University of California Gold Medal, is an Officer of the Order of Australia, a 'National Living Treasure', and is now the subject of a 55-cent Australian stamp. He lives with his wife, Judith, in Manly in Sydney and is still writing.

DAN KIERAN is the co-founder and CEO of Unbound, the award-winning crowdfunding publishing platform that brings authors and readers together. He is the author of twelve books, including the *Sunday Times* bestseller *Crap Towns* – the first viral internet phenomenon to turn into a bestselling book – *The Idle Traveller* and *Three Men in a Float*, also recorded for BBC Radio 4. He has given talks on a range of subjects including fundraising, entrepreneurship, making surfboards and 'how to have ideas' for places like the Do Lectures and the European Parliament.

NEAL LAYTON is an award-winning illustrator and author of children's books. He has illustrated more than eighty titles to date, working with authors such as Children's Laureates Michael Rosen and Cressida Cowell, and won several prizes including a Gold Award for *That Rabbit Belongs to Emily Brown*. He also writes his own books including the pop-up book *The Story of Everything* and the bestselling *Mammoth Academy* series. His books are currently in print in more than sixteen languages worldwide. He lives in Portsmouth with his wife and two daughters.

ANTHONY McGOWAN is best known for his critically acclaimed fiction for young adults, including *The Knife That Killed Me*, which was made into a film in 2014, and *The Truth of Things* sequence, the third of which, *Rook*, was shortlisted for the Carnegie Medal in 2018, and the fourth, *Lark*, won the Carnegie Medal in 2020. He has also written novels and non-fiction for adults, including *The Art of Failing* and *How to Teach Philosophy to Your Dog*. He was born in Manchester, brought up in Leeds and lives in London.

GREGORY MAGUIRE is the author of nearly forty books for adults and children. His best-known work is *Wicked*, which inspired the blockbuster musical of the same name, now playing its sixteenth year on Broadway and nearly as many years in the West End in London. *After Alice, Confessions of an Ugly Stepsister, Mirror Mirror, Hiddensee, Matchless* and *A Wild Winter Swan* draw inspiration, variously, from Lewis Carroll, Perrault, the Brothers Grimm, E.T.A. Hoffman and Hans Christian Andersen. Maguire has written and performed original material for National Public Radio's 'All Things Considered' and is an occasional contributor to the *New York Times Book Review*. He lives in New England and in France.

AYISHA MALIK is the author of *Sofia Khan is Not Obliged* and *The Other Half of Happiness*. She has contributed to the YA anthology *A Change is Gonna Come*, a compilation of short stories and poems by BAME authors, and she was a WHSmith Fresh Talent Pick in 2016. *Sofia Khan* was chosen for World Book Night and was a London CityReads choice in May 2019. Ayisha has been shortlisted for the Asian Women of Achievement Award, *Marie Claire*'s Future Shapers Awards and h100's Awards for Publishing and Writing. She is also the ghost-writer for Great British Bake Off winner, Nadiya Hussain. Ayisha's third novel, *This Green and Pleasant Land*, has been optioned for television.

JAMES MAYHEW has been creating books for children for over thirty years, from the *Katie* art series to *Ella Bella Ballerina*. He has also collaborated with many other writers and illustrators, including Joyce Dunbar (*Mouse and Mole*), Jackie Morris and most recently Zeb Soanes for *Gaspard the Fox*. He has won several prizes, including the *New York Times* Award in 1994. Alongside his work in publishing, James also presents classical concerts with art created live on stage. His collaborators include the Doric String Quartet and the BBC National Orchestra of Wales. He lives in Suffolk, where the big skies and gentle light are perfect for illustrating.

WYL MENMUIR is a novelist, editor and literary consultant based in Cornwall. His first novel, *The Many*, was nominated for the Man-Booker Prize 2016 and was an Observer Best Fiction of the Year pick. His short fiction and essays have appeared in *Best British Short Stories*, *Elementum* and *Pipeline*. Wyl now lives on Cornwall's north coast with his wife and two children. He is co-creator of the Cornish writing centre, 'The Writers' Block', and works with the Arvon Foundation, National Literacy Trust and Centre for Literacy in Primary Education on national literacy programmes, as well as being a lecturer in creative writing at Falmouth University and Manchester Metropolitan University.

KIRAN MILLWOOD HARGRAVE's bestselling debut *The Girl of Ink & Stars* won the Waterstones Children's Book Prize and the British Book Awards Children's Book of the Year in 2017. Her second, *The Island at the End of Everything*, was shortlisted for the Blue Peter Award and the Costa Children's Book Award. Her third title for children is *The Way Past Winter*, and her debut book for grown-ups, *The Mercies*, is published by Picador. She lives in Oxford with her husband, the artist Tom de Freston, and their cat, Luna.

DAVID MITCHELL is the author of six novels, including *Cloud Atlas*, *The Thousand Autumns of Jacob de Zoet*, *The Bone Clocks* and, most recently, *Utopia Avenue*. His books have been translated into over thirty languages, adapted for films and have received a number of UK and international awards. In recent years he has also written opera libretti, TV and film scripts, and is the co-translator of the bestselling books about life with autism by Japanese author Naoki Higashida. As the Future Library Project's inductee of 2016, he submitted a novella – *From Me Flows What You Call Time* – that will not be published until 2114. He lives in Ireland.

JAN MORRIS is a celebrated author and historian, whose adventurous life of writing and travel notably began with an assignment to cover the 1953 Everest expedition for *The Times*. She is an Honorary DLitt of the University of Wales, a member of the Gordedd of Bards and an Honorary Student of her old Oxford college, Christ Church. Her books include *Coronation Everest, Venice, The Pax Britannica Trilogy, Conundrum, Trieste and the Meaning of Nowhere* and *Wales, Epic Views of a Small Country. A Writer's World*, a collection of her travel writing and reportage from over five decades, was published in 2003 and her novel *Hav*, published in a new and expanded form in 2006, was shortlisted for the Booker Prize. *The Times* has named her one of the greatest British writers since the War.

SARAH MOSS is the author of six novels, the latest of which is *Ghost Wall*, and a memoir of a year in Iceland. She was born in Glasgow, grew up in Manchester and moved between Oxford, Reykjavik, West Cornwall and now the West Midlands, where she is Professor of Creative Writing at the University of Warwick.

BENJAMIN MYERS is an award-winning author, poet and journalist. His novels include *The Gallows Pole* (winner of the Walter Scott Prize), *Beastings* (the Portico Prize for Literature) and *Pig Iron* (the Gordon Burn Prize). He has also published the non-fiction work *Under the Rock* and his most recent novel *The Offing* is published by Bloomsbury.

BEVERLEY NAIDOO began writing in Britain while working as a teacher. *Journey to Jo'burg* was banned in her native South Africa until 1991. She has written novels, short stories, picture books and plays and has edited anthologies. Her work for young people has been widely translated and has received many international and UK awards, including the Carnegie Medal for *The Other Side of Truth*. Adult non-fiction includes *Through Whose Eyes?*, based on her PhD, and *Death of an Idealist: In Search of Neil Aggett*, a biography of a young doctor-cum-trade unionist who died in apartheid detention. She lives in Bournemouth.

SALLY NICHOLLS was born in Stockton, just after midnight, in a thunderstorm. At the age of twenty-two she enrolled on an MA in Writing for Young People at the University of Bath Spa, where she wrote her first novel, *Ways to Live Forever*. She has won many awards, including the Waterstones Children's Book Prize, the Glen Dimplex New Writer of the

Year (children's category and overall winner) and the Independent Bookshop Week (IBW) Book Award. Her YA novel about the suffrage movement, *Things a Bright Girl Can Do* was shortlisted for a Carnegie, and *An Island of Our Own* was shortlisted for the Costa Book of the Year and the *Guardian* Children's Fiction Prize. Her books have been translated into over twenty languages, and *Ways to Live Forever* was made into a feature film. Sally lives in Oxford and spends her time writing stories and looking after her two small children.

PARAIC O'DONNELL is a novelist and critic. His debut novel, *The Maker of Swans*, was shortlisted for the Irish Book Awards in the Newcomer of the Year category. His second, *The House on Vesper Sands*, was a *Guardian* and *Observer* Book of the Year in 2018. His essays and reviews have appeared in the *Irish Times*, *Guardian*, *Winter Papers* and elsewhere. He lives in Wicklow, Ireland.

CHIBUNDU ONUZO is a Nigerian novelist. Her first novel, *The Spider King's Daughter*, won a Betty Trask Award, was shortlisted for the Dylan Thomas Prize and the Commonwealth Book Prize, and was longlisted for the Desmond Elliott Prize and the Etisalat Prize for Literature. Her most recent novel, *Welcome to Lagos*, was published in 2017 and has been reprinted three times. In 2018 Onuzo was elected Fellow of the Royal Society of Literature in its '40 Under 40' initiative.

ONJALI Q. RAÚF is the author of *The Boy at the Back of the Class*, her debut novel highlighting the plight of refugee children, which won the Waterstones Children's Book Prize and the Blue Peter Book Awards 2019, and was also nominated for the Carnegie Medal and shortlisted for the Jhalak Prize 2019. Her second book, *The Star Outside My Window*, not only touches on the issue of domestic violence but also her failed aspirations to become an astronomer. She lives in London and believes at least 75 per cent of her body mass is made up of chocolate and stardust (and the other 25 per cent of tea).

CHRIS RIDDELL is a graphic artist, author and political cartoonist whose illustrations have brought him wide acclaim, a UNESCO Award and the Children's Laureateship. He is the first ever illustrator to win the Kate Greenaway Medal three times, most recently for his illustrations of Neil Gaiman's *The Sleeper and the Spindle*. His first *Goth Girl* novel won the Costa Children's Book Award in 2013. Together with Paul Stewart he is the creator of the hugely successful *Edge Chronicles*, *Barnaby Grimes* and the award-winning *Far-Flung Adventures*. He lives in Brighton.

ANDY RILEY is an Emmy-winning scriptwriter, cartoonist and children's author. His sixteen books include the *Bunny Suicides* series, the *King Flashypants* series and *Great Lies To Tell Small Kids*. His scriptwriting credits include *Veep*, *Year of The Rabbit*, *Little Britain*, *Armstrong and Miller*, *Smack the Pony*, *The Armando Iannucci Shows*, *Gnomeo & Juliet*, *Tracey Ullman's Show*, *The Boy in the Dress*, *The Great Outdoors*, *Hyperdrive*, *Gangsta Granny*, *Come Fly with Me*, *Big Train*, *Graham Norton*, *Spitting Image*, *The 99p Challenge* and BAFTA-winning episodes of *Black Books* and *Robbie the Reindeer*.

MICHAEL ROSEN is a hugely bestselling author and poet, who has now created over 140 books. His first job was as a Christmas chicken-plucker. Since 2014 he has been Professor of Children's Literature at Goldsmiths, University of London. He is today best known as a broadcaster on BBC Radio 4's *Word of Mouth* and author of the perennial favourite *We're Going on a Bear Hunt*, illustrated by Helen Oxenbury; they celebrated its 25th anniversary in 2014 by breaking a Guinness World Record for the 'Largest Reading Lesson', an event attended by 1,500 children and live-streamed online to more than 30,000 children across the country. He was the Children's Laureate for 2007–9 and the winner of the Eleanor Farjeon Award. He lives in London.

JACOB ROSS is a novelist, short story writer, editor and tutor of Narrative Craft. His crime fiction novel *The Bone Readers* won the inaugural Jhalak Prize in 2017. His literary novel *Pynter Bender* was published to critical acclaim and was shortlisted for the 2009 Commonwealth Writers' Regional Prize and chosen as one of the British Authors' Club Best First Novels. His most recent novel, *Black Rain Falling*, was published in 2020. Film and television rights to his *Camaho Quartet* series have been acquired by Neon Ink Productions.

LORNA SCOBIE grew up in the English countryside, which has led to her obsession with the natural world. She has illustrated a number of books for children, often with a focus on animals and the environment, as well as a bestselling series on everyday creativity. When not spending time watering her own forest of house plants, Lorna can be found among fellow designers in the children's book team at Macmillan. Her first author-illustrated picture book, *Collecting Cats*, published in 2019.

ANDY SHEPHERD is the author of *The Boy Who Grew Dragons* series, the first book of which was shortlisted for the Waterstones Children's Prize and the Sheffield Children's Book Award and was longlisted for the Blue Peter Book Award 2019. Her books have sold in thirteen countries and are being developed for television. She lives near Cambridge and having grown up on the coast, messing about in boats (and mud) she spends most of her spare time trying to work out how to move this beautiful city closer to the sea. Disclaimer: all dragon-growing is undertaken entirely at the grower's own risk and Andy cannot be held responsible for any damage your dragon may cause.

FRANCESCA SIMON is the author of the hugely popular *Horrid Henry* series, which has sold over 21 million copies and is published in twenty-nine countries. She has written more than fifty books and won the Children's Book of the Year in 2008 at the British Book Awards for *Horrid Henry and the Abominable Snowman*. Her books for older children include *The Sleeping Army* and *The Lost Gods*, and her first book for teens, *The Monstrous Child*, about Hel, the Norse goddess of the dead, was shortlisted for both the 2017 Costa Book Awards and the YA Book Prize. She wrote the libretto for an opera based on *The Monstrous Child* with the composer Gavin Higgins, which premiered at the Royal Opera House in February 2019. She went to Yale and Oxford universities, where she studied medieval literature, art history and Anglo-Saxon. She lives in London with her family.

CHITRA SOUNDAR is an Indian-born British author and storyteller based in London. She has written over forty books for children, published across Asia, Europe and North America. Her *Farmer Falgu* series was included in the USBBY list of International books in 2019, has won numerous accolades and has been translated into many languages. She had four new books out in 2019 in the UK and the US, ranging from fiction to non-fiction.

ANDY STANTON is the author of the popular children's series *Mr Gum*, which has been translated into more than thirty languages and won numerous awards, including the inaugural Roald Dahl Funny Prize. In addition he has written picture books including *Here Comes the Poo Bus!*, *Going to the Volcano* and *Danny McGee Drinks the Sea*. In 2019 he launched a new middle-grade series, *The Paninis of Pompeii*, and adapted *Mr Gum and the Dancing Bear* into a successful stage musical for the National Theatre. He lives in north London.

HELEN STEPHENS has been writing and illustrating picture books for over twenty years. She is best known for her *How to Hide a Lion* series which was nominated for the CILIP Kate Greenaway Medal, and has been translated into nearly twenty languages. It was adapted for stage by the Polka Theatre, and toured the UK in 2019. She taught on the MA course Illustrating for Children at Anglia Ruskin University and is currently a Picture Hooks mentor. She started the Instagram hashtag project #walktosee for drawings from life. It has contributions from sketchbookers all over the world.

COLIN THUBRON is an acclaimed travel writer and novelist, and the winner of many prizes and awards. His first books were about the Middle East – Damascus, Lebanon and Cyprus. In 1982 he travelled by car into the Soviet Union, a journey described in *Among the Russians*. From these early experiences developed his classic travel books: *Behind the Wall* (winner of the Hawthornden Prize and the Thomas Cook Travel Award), *The Lost Heart of Asia*, *In Siberia* (Prix Bouvier), *Shadow of the Silk Road* and *To a Mountain in Tibet*. He was awarded CBE in 2007, and between 2008 and 2017 was President of the Royal Society of Literature. He is currently working on a book about the Amur river.

PIERS TORDAY lives in London but longs to be out walking in the Northumberland woods. His bestselling first book, *The Last Wild*, was shortlisted for the Waterstones Children's Book Prize and nominated for the CILIP Carnegie Medal. His second, *The Dark Wild*, won the *Guardian* Children's Fiction Prize 2014. Other books include *The Wild Beyond*, *There May Be A Castle*, *The Lost Magician* and *The Frozen Sea*, and he also completed his father Paul Torday's final book, *The Death of an Owl*. His adaptation of John Masefield's *The Box of Delights* opened at Wilton's Music Hall in 2017. His latest play is a retelling of the Dickens festive classic *Christmas Carol*, which featured the first ever female Scrooge on the London stage; it opened at Wilton's in December 2019.

NOVUYO ROSA TSHUMA is the author of *House of Stone*, winner of the 2019 Edward Stanford Travel Writing Award for Fiction and the 2019 Bulawayo Arts Award for Outstanding Fiction. In 2017 she received the Rockefeller Foundation's prestigious Bellagio Center Literary Arts Residency Award for her work. Her collection, *Shadows*, was published by Kwela in South Africa to critical acclaim and won the 2014 Herman Charles Bosman Prize. A graduate of the Iowa Writers' Workshop, she is a native of Zimbabwe and has lived in South Africa and the USA. Novuyo serves on the Editorial Advisory Board and is an editor at *The Bare Life Review*, a journal of refugee and immigrant literature based in California.

IRVINE WELSH is the author of many books of fiction, the first of which was *Trainspotting*, the latest *Dead Men's Trousers*. He writes film and TV scripts, largely with Dean Cavanagh. Since Danny Boyle's film adaptation of *Trainspotting* was released in 1996, Welsh has remained a controversial figure, whose novels, stage and screen plays, novellas and short stories have proved difficult for literary critics to assimilate, a difficulty made only more noticeable by his continued commercial success. *Trainspotting* has now sold almost a million copies in the UK alone and is a worldwide phenomenon. *Ecstasy* became the first paperback original to go straight in at the top of the *Sunday Times* bestseller list, a feat emulated by *Filth*. Books such as *Glue*, *Porno* and the recent *The Bedroom Secrets of the Master Chefs* have seen his profile rise in America and Canada. He lives mainly in Dublin but retreats to Miami Beach for a large part of the winter.

ADAM WEYMOUTH is a writer and journalist. His first book, *Kings of the Yukon*, won the *Sunday Times* Young Writer of the Year and the Lonely Planet Adventure Travel Book of the Year. It tells the story of a 2,000-mile canoe trip across Canada and Alaska, charting the decline of the king salmon and the impact their decline is having on the many people and ecosystems that depend on them. He lives on a 100-year-old Dutch barge on the River Lea in London.

RAYNOR WINN's debut non-fiction book, *The Salt Path*, was shortlisted for the Wainwright Prize, the Costa Biography Award, an Edward Stanford Travel Writing Award and received the Royal Society of Literature's Christopher Bland Prize. Her second non-fiction work, *The Wild Silence*, was published in 2020. She lives in Cornwall.

EMMA YARLETT is an award-winning illustrator, baker and picture book maker. She graduated from University College Falmouth in 2011 and has since created animations for the Waterstones Children's Book Prize and illustrated non-fiction for Julia Donaldson. Her work includes *Orion and the Dark*, *Poppy Pickle* and a bestselling series about the book monster *Nibbles*. She now paints, draws, collages, designs, doodles, splatters and sketches for a living from her home in Cornwall.

Acknowledgments

Everyone has a different approach. If you want to become a writer you do have to *write*, which is obvious enough, and persevere to get through the bad and the good. As Hemingway put it: 'I write one page of masterpiece to ninety-one pages of shit. I try to put the shit in the wastebasket.'

My students often ask me about *being* a writer and, truth be told, I'm still making it up as I go along. So what do I know? Read. Write. Repeat. Make lists. Start over. That's how it goes for me. Be hopeful and practical too. Take off your shoes. I'd say that's solid advice for most types of life. I try to encourage my students to be tenacious. To be creative. And to be kind.

In teaching, this book emerged. I thought of it as a useful primer for my students, as much as something to help me too, and it was a privilege to be able to reach out to authors whose work I admire. The book took shape talking to some fellow writer friends and slowly, by looking and listening, the project grew into this collection, which found the right home at the right moment with the British Library. It would be nothing without the insights of the writers who willingly joined in and so to all of you, and to your readers, we say a large and genuine *thank you*.

This book is basically just one big list. Let's call it a productive procrastination. Being swallowed by this particular whale has helped me as a writer. I feel consoled and inspired in new ways. At the Library, my old friend John Lee is now leading the publications team. Thanks as always to my ongoing-marvel-of-an-editor Sarah Vernon-Hunt, design guru Karin Fremer and Bill Bragg, who applied his craft to another top jacket. And daily gratitude to Kari for giving me the time to write and the peace to read.

I hope there's more to come. Tomorrow, after 'remote teaching' the last of this year's students in my kitchen, I'll be researching a pair of pioneering birdwatchers. My first children's book is out soon, a simple story about an annoying apple. I have a PhD in icebergs and I'm writing about fruit. And why not.

Outside, the world spins. The climate is in crisis and many of our leaders appear to have come from another planet. A coronavirus begins its cruel spread. Routines have been turned upside down. Freedoms restricted. Lives cut short. As I write this, no one has any clear idea when the fatal chapter will end. Brave doctors and nurses take up the fight. We look out the window. We clap and we hope. We have more than books to read. We must relearn to live.

Huw Lewis-Jones, Cornwall

Further Reading

Read the best books first,
or you may not have a chance to read them all.
HENRY DAVID THOREAU

'Books are made out of books,' said Cormac McCarthy, when pressed by a journalist to reveal his literary influences. There are just so many books that could be useful to you when embarking on a book of your own. Ask yourself the simplest of questions. What do you want to create? What's the idea? Where to begin?

Well, if you're still here, and you really can't face the actual writing bit just yet, then you can probably anticipate what I'm going to say to you now: *read anything you like*. It's that simple! And then read some more. And then, even more importantly, read some things you think that you're not going to like. You might surprise yourself and, at the very least, you'll settle more on the kind of writing that works for you.

As Terry Pratchett put it: 'Read widely outside the genre. Read about the Old West (a fantasy in itself) or Georgian London or how Nelson's navy was victualled or the history of alchemy or clock making or the mail coach system. Read with the mind-set of a carpenter looking at trees.' Helpful? Maybe not if you're writing another picture book about a crocodile (which is just what I'm doing), but reading like this would surely take you on an unfamiliar path, and who knows at this stage if this is where you need to be heading? That's what creativity is. Ramble about in unusual directions. Find inspiration where you least expect it. Let yourself get lost at every opportunity. You'll make your way back home soon enough.

Or, try a different approach. Why not set yourself the goal of reading one book from each of our contributors? Their short biographies should give you the start you need to escape into their books. There are more than sixty incredible writers here, and a huge variety of styles and interests. But perhaps you just want more inspiration on the writing process itself, or other books that describe the ways that different creatives go about their practice? Well, here are twenty more I've enjoyed for all kinds of reasons:

Lynda Barry, *What It Is* (Drawn and Quarterly, 2008)
Brian Bilston, *Diary of a Somebody* (Picador, 2019)
Julia Cameron, *The Artist's Way* (Macmillan, 2016)
Kate Clanchy, *Some Kids I Taught and What They Taught Me* (Picador, 2019)
Daniel Eatock, *Imprint* (Princeton, 2008)

Grant Faulkner, *Pep Talks for Writers* (Chronicle, 2017)

Neil Gaiman, *Art Matters* (Headline, 2018)

Maira Kalman, *The Principles of Uncertainty* (Penguin, 2009)

Stephen King, *On Writing* (Hodder, 2012)

Austin Kleon, *Steal Like an Artist* (Workman, 2012)

Anne Lamott, *Bird by Bird* (Anchor, 1995)

Ursula Le Guin, *Steering the Craft* (Mariner, 2015)

Elmore Leonard, *Elmore Leonard's 10 Rules of Writing* (Morrow, 2007)

Betsy Lerner, *The Forest for the Trees* (Riverhead, 2010)

Jonathan Lethem, *The Ecstasy of Influence* (Doubleday, 2011)

Sidney Lumet, *Making Movies* (Bloomsbury, 1996)

Colum McCann, *Letters to a Young Writer* (Bloomsbury, 2017)

Scott McCloud, *Understanding Comics* (HarperPerennial, 2001)

Hugh MacLeod, *Ignore Everybody* (Portfolio 2009)

John McPhee, *Draft No. 4* (Farrar, 2017)

Philip Pullman, *Daemon Voices* (David Fickling, 2017)

Kio Stark, *Don't Go Back to School* (Greenglass, 2013)

Kurt Vonnegut, *If This Isn't Nice, What Is?* (Seven Stories, 2016)

That's twenty-three, I realize. It's hard to choose. As with everything in this book, feel free to take what advice you like. Dive in and don't fear the whale. Make your own rules. Your stories might start in distant places, inspired by memories of times past, sparked by new ideas and informed by all the many books you've read, even things that are only half-remembered or long-forgotten.

Stories are inside all of us, even if we don't realize or appreciate that fact; we should take time to stop and listen to what our hearts and our minds might be telling us. They're in our DNA as humans: from tales told around the fire thousands of years ago, to the next time you see a friend and chat about your day and your hopes for the future. Once upon a time – as stories begin in our many languages – long, long ago, beyond the nine mountains and the seven rivers, when all the tigers smoked long pipes, on a dark and stormy night, in a galaxy far, far away …

Beyond all this, know that to become a writer you really must learn to love being a reader. The last word goes to William Faulkner: 'Read, read, read. Read everything – trash, classics, good and bad, and see how they do it. Just like a carpenter who works as an apprentice and studies the master. Read! You'll absorb it. Then write. If it is good, you'll find out. If it's not, throw it out the window.'

PROCRASTINATION FOR CREATIVE WRITERS, A 10-WEEK COURSE

TOPICS COVERED INCLUDE:

- WORKSPACE ARRANGEMENT
- PRE-WRITING RITUALS
- STATIONERY CHOICES
- WAITING FOR INSPIRATION
- SNACKS AND BEVERAGES
- FINDING THE PERFECT FONT
- WORKSPACE REARRANGEMENT
- UTILIZING SOCIAL MEDIA
- PAUSES, TEA BREAKS AND NAPS
- ADVANCED WORKSPACE REARRANGEMENT

BOOK NOW   SHARE

Kwame Alexander Jim Al-Khalili David
Badoe Harry Baker Alex Bell Sita Brah
Chevalier Frank Cottrell-Boyce Cre
Maz Evans Simon Garfield Tom Gauld Le
Harris Michelle Harrison Philip Hoar
Jensen Catherine Johnson Thomas Kenea
Anthony McGowan Gregory Maguire Ayi
Millwood Hargrave David Mitchell Jan
Naidoo Sally Nicholls Paraic O'Donn
Riddell Andy Riley Michael Rosen Jacob
Simon Chitra Soundar Andy Stanton He
Novuyo Rosa Tshuma Irvine Welsh A
Kwame Alexander Jim Al-Khalili David
Badoe Harry Baker Alex Bell Sita Brah
Chevalier Frank Cottrell-Boyce Cre
Maz Evans Simon Garfield Tom Gauld Le
Harris Michelle Harrison Philip Hoar
Jensen Catherine Johnson Thomas Kenea
Anthony McGowan Gregory Maguire Ayi
Millwood Hargrave David Mitchell Jan
Naidoo Sally Nicholls Paraic O'Donn
Riddell Andy Riley Michael Rosen Jacob
Simon Chitra Soundar Andy Stanton He
Novuyo Rosa Tshuma Irvine Welsh A
Kwame Alexander Jim Al-Khalili David
Badoe Harry Baker Alex Bell Sita Brah
Chevalier Frank Cottrell-Boyce Cre
Maz Evans Simon Garfield Tom Gauld Le
Harris Michelle Harrison Philip Hoar
Jensen Catherine Johnson Thomas Kenea
Anthony McGowan Gregory Maguire Ayi
Millwood Hargrave David Mitchell Jan
Naidoo Sally Nicholls Paraic O'Donn
Riddell Andy Riley Michael Rosen Jacob
Simon Chitra Soundar Andy Stanton He
Novuyo Rosa Tshuma Irvine Welsh